Ritual of

ROYALTY

The Ceremony and Pageantry of Britain's Monarchy

Michèle Brown

PRENTICE-HALL, INC.
Englewood Cliffs, N.J.

First published in the United States of America in 1983
by Prentice Hall, Inc.
Originally published in Great Britain in 1983
by Sidgwick and Jackson Limited

Designed by James Campus
Picture Research by Philippa Lewis
Maps by Katharina Kelly

Library of Congress Catalog Number 82-063122
ISBN 0-13-781047-4 (hardcover)
ISBN 0-13-781039-3 (softcover)

Phototypeset in Monophoto Modern by
Green Gates Studios, Hull
Printed in Great Britain by
Hazell Watson and Viney Limited,
Aylesbury, Bucks

FOR GYLES

The Author would like to thank the following: Colin
Cole, Garter King of Arms; Major R. A. G. Courage,
Household Division; Malcolm R. Innes of Edingight,
Lord Lyon King of Arms; Major General G. H. Mills,
Resident Governor and Keeper of the Jewel House, H.M.
Tower of London; Sergeant-Major H. C. Phillips, The
Yeomen of the Guard; Michael Raymer, Assistant
Secretary, Royal Hospital Chelsea; Conrad Swan, York
Herald of Arms and Genealogist, Order of the Bath; and
all the other numerous individuals and bodies who
helped with the research for this book. Any opinions
expressed are, of course, mine, and so are any mistakes.
Thanks also to Ann O'Connor, Paul James and my
editor, Libby Joy.

ALSO BY MICHÈLE BROWN

Food by Appointment
The Little Royal Book
Queen Elizabeth II: *The Silver Jubilee Book*
Pears Royal Year Book
Prince Charles
Prince Charles and Lady Diana
Restoration and Repair
Restoring Old Junk
The Royal Animals
The Silver Jubilee Diary

Contents

PICTURE ACKNOWLEDGEMENTS

The picture on page 20 is reproduced by Gracious permission of Her Majesty the Queen and the pictures on pages 15 and 104 by courtesy of the Dean and Chapter of Westminster Abbey. Other photographs and illustrations were supplied by, or are reproduced by kind permission of, the following: The British Library, 102, 105 (*left*); The British Museum, 82 (*top and bottom*) (photos Ray Gardner), 108–9 (photos J. Freeman); Camera Press, 26, 163, 170; Crown Copyright, reproduced with permission of the Controller of H.M.S.O., 63, 76, 87 (photo on loan from Royal Hospital Chelsea); Fox Photos, 68; Guildhall Library, City of London, 46–7. 114; Keystone Press, 34 (Collection, Yeomen of the Guard), 45, 136; The Mansell Collection, 14, 19, 22, 24, 31, 58, 83 (*left and right*), 162; National Army Museum, 18, 40, 42, 51, 57, 62, 69; Popperfoto, 72, 90, 115, 118, 123; Press Association, 165 (*right*); Radio Times Hulton Picture Library, 12 (*left and right*), 17, 25, 79, 105 (*right*), 122, 128, 138, 140, 148 (*left and right*), 149, 152, 158, 169; Royal Hospital Chelsea, 88; The Scotsman, 53, 111; Scottish Tourist Board, 130; Syndication International, 144, 165 (*left*); The Times, 94, 95 (on loan from Guildhall Library); Victoria and Albert Museum, 100; Collection, Yeomen of the Guard, 36.

COLOUR PICTURES

Between pages 74 and 75: page i, Andy Kyle/Camera Press (*top*) and Dick Makin (*bottom, left and right*); page ii, the Household Division (*top and bottom*); page iii, Angelo Hornak; page iv, The British Library and (*inset*) the Household Division.

Between pages 154 and 155: page i, the Household Division (*top*) and The British Library (*bottom*); page ii, Scottish Tourist Board (*top and bottom left*) and Lionel Cherruault/Camera Press (*bottom right*); page iii, Fox Photos; page iv, Daily Express.

Introduction

In Britain the Crown, in the person of the Queen, is the Head of State and the focus of national unity. Now that real power is in the hands of the Prime Minister and the government it is the symbolic nature of the monarchy which has become predominant and this is most evident in the ceremonies and rituals of State. Most of our ceremonial is connected with the monarchy and from time to time it is criticized as being expensive, outmoded, and possibly ridiculous. Yet to criticize these ceremonies is to ignore the fact that human beings run a great part of their lives on the basis of little rituals. Even such everyday events as shaking hands or making a cup of tea are part of the same general scheme of things as a Coronation or the State Opening of Parliament. We know we find shaking hands reassuring, just as most people find the repetition of royal rituals and ceremonies reassuring, yet often we do not know why. We instinctively know that to shake hands is a gesture of friendship though we may not know that it derives from the time when men fought with swords, generally held in the right hand, and by clasping another man's right hand with yours you demonstrated that you were not about to strike him.

So royal ceremonial, which may be superficially meaningless and unattractive to those who dislike too much pomp and pageantry, is generally founded on quite sensible premises. For example a Royal Gun Salute is rather like a handshake – by emptying the gun in a salute you prove you have no ammunition left with which to fire on your visitor! The purpose of this book is to explain not only the ceremonies themselves but the background to them; knowing the significance of apparently meaningless, if attractive, events like Beating Retreat makes them much more interesting to watch.

Although our national ceremonies are often associated with the Queen and the Royal Family the examples of countries which have never had, or decided to do without, a monarchy do not indicate that no monarchy means no ceremony. Quite the reverse, in fact – as anyone who has watched the ceremonial which is associated with running the Stars and Stripes up the flagpole in the United States, or who has seen pictures of the May Day parade in Red Square, must agree. However it manifests itself, ritual and ceremony, even pomp and pageantry, seem to answer a vital need felt by the majority of human beings. Family customs, local customs, and national ceremony all interweave into a firm mesh which gives us at least the illusion that life is all of a piece and not just a random assortment of daily events. For many people much of the solace derived from religion comes from the soothing repetition of the ritual. To be cynical about these rituals, any of which, out of context, can be made to appear ludicrous, is to fail to understand how human beings organize themselves.

In Britain our royal ceremonies, though they have the disadvantage in one way that they are associated so closely with one small group of people, have the corresponding advantage that they are easier to feel involved with precisely because they are so personal. And there is no feeling that what was meaningful once may never be changed. In the twentieth century many alterations have been made in the formality which surrounds the monarchy. Richard Crossman, in his *Diaries of a Cabinet Minister*, pointed out some of the slightly ridiculous anachronisms which have lingered on, especially those which he came across as Lord President of the Council – the wearing of Court Dress with its old-fashioned knee breeches and black stockings, the necessity of walking backwards out of the Sovereign's presence. To his surprise the Queen was quite prepared to consider change when anachronisms were pointed out to her. On the other hand when Crossman wished to be excused from attending the State Opening of Parliament the Queen's Private Secretary explained that many such public ceremonies were a chore for the Queen herself and that while she might be prepared to excuse him from attendance she might be tempted to ask herself why he should be let off when she could not be. Crossman took the matter no further but chose to attend the ceremony; like the Queen, he realized that ritual has its place in government.

Such ceremonies may be a sum of rather incomprehensible parts but by their constant repetition and attention to detail they underline the continuity of the system of Parliamentary democracy in which the Crown, although no longer holding real political power, is the symbolic head both of the government and of the nation which is governed. It is this apparent contradiction which makes the system work smoothly. To erode away the form would be to show a contempt for the system it represents, a system which has already proved it works well and flexibly.

The success of the monarchical system, demonstrated through its ceremonial, is enhanced by the members of the Royal Family themselves, and by their response to what is required of them at different times. The Queen, who is punctilious in the observance of traditional ceremonies, has willingly seen the end of Presentation parties at Court which served no useful function in post-war society. On the other hand some ancient ceremonies whose meaning is as important today as ever, such as the Royal Maundy, have been revived and given new emphasis.

One of the major advantages of royal ceremonial over anything which might take its place is that it has stood the test of time. It is flexible and usually based in good ideas which may have become rather obscure but which nevertheless allow them to be performed with sincerity. Because the ceremony and the pageantry help to make the Crown more attractive to the people they strengthen it, and so paradoxically what was once the symbol of autocratic rule becomes itself a power for curbing the excesses of government.

The crowds who are attracted to royal ceremonies, and even to occasions where there is nothing to be seen but the Queen herself, are a strong indication of the continuing attraction of the institution and of the function it fulfils in giving a little zest to our lives while providing a living focus for the nation's sense of unity. It was neatly summed up by Winston Churchill when he described the wedding of Princess Elizabeth and the Duke of Edinburgh in 1947 as 'A flash of colour on the hard road we have to travel'. Television has helped to bring all these events into our homes but there is still nothing to compare with being present in person on an occasion such as Trooping the Colour or a royal wedding. This book therefore includes details of times and places for all those who like to experience their pageantry at first hand. There may be a serious purpose behind the time-honoured 'rituals of royalty' but the success of that purpose depends on their being not just understood but enjoyed by as many people as possible.

Accession

The period after the death of a monarch is a time of national mourning. Yet for a few hours that mourning officially ceases while the nation expresses its joy at the succession of a new Sovereign and proclaims the Accession in towns throughout the land. Before the new Sovereign can be proclaimed there is one formality which must be observed. Although the monarchy is now largely viewed as an efficiently working part of government as a whole, the goodwill of the new King or Queen cannot be taken for granted. Before the Accession can be officially proclaimed the Sovereign must appear before the Accession Council, a group of Privy Councillors and other elder statesmen and women and peers of the realm. There the new Sovereign takes the Oath of Succession, which, since it dates back to a time of religious controversy and fear of the Crown being taken over by foreigners and 'papists', consists largely in swearing to maintain the Protestant Church of England and of Scotland.

Even though this is now a formality the procedure is strictly adhered to. When George vi died in 1952 his daughter, Princess Elizabeth, was on an official tour of Kenya. Until she could be contacted and flown back to London to take her oath before the Accession Council she could not be proclaimed, and there was an uncharacteristic delay of some forty-eight hours between the announcement of the King's death on 6 February and the Proclamation of the new Queen Elizabeth ii on 8 February.

The Proclamation is read in several towns throughout the country, including Edinburgh and Cardiff. In London the Proclamation is read four times in all, twice in the City of Westminster and twice in the City of London, which was once a dangerously independent area which needed to be reminded of its duty to its Sovereign.

The first reading of the Proclamation takes place from the balcony of St James's Palace which overlooks Friary Court. There are good historical reasons for this and St James's Palace is still the official location of the Court.

In the sixteenth century Henry viii dissolved the monasteries, which were extremely wealthy, and kept much of their property for his own use. One of these properties was the site of St James's monastery. Henry needed a new palace after the destruction of the Palace of Westminster by fire, and the St James's site was ideal. The palace he built there, together with the London residence of Cardinal Wolsey, who had forfeited his property when he had fallen into disgrace, became the King's main residences. The former was known as St James's Palace and the latter was given the new name of Whitehall. Whitehall was burned down in 1698, although the famous Banqueting Hall designed by Inigo Jones, with ceiling paintings by Rubens, still exists. As a result St James's became the principal London residence of the monarch. At the end of the eighteenth century George III acquired Buckingham Palace, which subsequently Queen Victoria chose as her principal London residence. Although every monarch since has followed her example, St James's has remained the official centre of the court. New ambassadors drive to see the Queen at Buckingham Palace so that they can be accredited to the Court of St James's!

Therefore when the clock had struck eleven on the morning of 8 February, it was on the balcony at St James's Palace that the Kings of Arms, the heralds, and pursuivants in all their medieval splendour, appeared with the Earl Marshal of England, the Duke of Norfolk. After a fanfare of trumpets Garter King of Arms read the following Proclamation to the waiting crowd:

Whereas it hath pleased Almighty God to call to His Mercy our late Sovereign Lord King George the Sixth of Blessed and Glorious Memory by whose Decease the Crown is solely and rightfully come to the High and Mighty Princess Elizabeth Alexandra Mary; We, therefore, the Lords Spiritual and Temporal of this Realm, being here assisted with these of His late Majesty's Privy Council, with representatives of other members of the Commonwealth, with the Principal Gentlemen of Quality, with the Lord Mayor, Aldermen and Citizens of London, do now hereby with one voice and Consent of Tongue and Heart publish and proclaim that the High and Mighty Princess Elizabeth Alexandra Mary is now, by the Death of our late Sovereign of Happy Memory, become Queen Elizabeth the Second, by the Grace of God Queen of this Realm and of all her other Realms and Territories, Head of the Commonwealth, Defender of the Faith, to whom Her lieges do acknowledge all Faith and constant Obedience, with hearty and humble Affection; beseeching God, by whom Kings and Queens do reign, to bless the Royal Princess Elizabeth the Second with long and happy years to reign over us.

As soon as the Proclamation had been read the Garter King of Arms raised his hat high in the air crying 'God Save the Queen!', a cry which was repeated by everyone else before the military band played the National Anthem. To mark the first reading of the Proclamation gun salutes were fired in Hyde Park and at the Tower of London.

Shortly afterwards the same group of heralds formed a carriage procession under the escort of the Household Cavalry to read the Proclamation first at Charing Cross, by the statue of Charles I which looks down Whitehall, and then in the City. Even on such a solemn occasion the procession had to wait at Temple Bar until formally admitted into the City by the Lord Mayor.

After the Proclamation was read at Temple Bar the procession moved further into the City to read it for the last time on the steps of the Royal Exchange. Each time there followed enthusiastic cries of 'God Save the Queen!'

Sir Gerald Woolaston, Norroy and Ulster King of Arms, proclaiming at Temple Bar the Accession of Edward VIII, January 1936 (*right*) and the Accession of Elizabeth II, February 1952 (*left*)

The reading of the Proclamation at Edinburgh and the other Scottish towns was delayed by a week to symbolize the time it used to take to carry the news on horseback north of the border. In Scotland such Proclamations are read by the senior Scottish Herald, the Lord Lyon King of Arms. In Edinburgh, as in London, the Proclamation is read four times, once at the Mercat Cross, once at the Gate of Edinburgh Castle, once in front of Holyroodhouse and once on the Pier and Shore of Leith.

A similar ceremony is always held a few months later for the Proclamation of the Coronation, when exactly the same procedure is adopted. The Proclamation of Elizabeth II's Coronation took place on 7 June 1952.

It will undoubtedly be many years before such a Proclamation is read again, but there is no reason to believe the procedure will vary in any way from that followed at the Accession of Elizabeth II.

Date **Within 48 hours of the death of a Sovereign. Within 7 days in Scotland. See the Press for details.**
Place **Four traditional places in London: St James's Palace, Charing Cross, Chancery Lane, and the Royal Exchange. Four traditional places in Scotland: Mercat Cross, Edinburgh Castle, Holyroodhouse, Pier and Shore of Leith.**
Time **See the Press for times (usually 11.00 a.m.)**

Where to stand **You need to arrive at least two hours in advance. Although only a short ceremony it happens so infrequently that many people try to witness it. Members of the public at past Proclamations have been allowed within a few feet of the Proclamation points, although the route is lined with the Brigade of Guards.**

Coronation

Stylized and formal recognition of a leader is not peculiar to this country or to this age. Well before the birth of Christ different societies such as the Egyptians and the Ancient Greeks performed ceremonies which gave their leaders an added mantle of authority greater than that to which they were entitled by birth or military prowess. Very often this ceremonial drew part of its authority from religious significance.

For nearly 2,000 years Western monarchies have used the Christian church to bolster up their power and impress on their subjects that obedience to temporal power is a spiritual duty. The same method was used thousands of years before by the kings of Egypt and the kings of Israel. There is a clear reminder of this in the anthem which was sung at the Coronation of Elizabeth II while she was being anointed by the Archbishop of Canterbury. This was 'Zadok the Priest and Nathan the Prophet anointed Solomon King'. The best-known musical setting of this is Handel's version written for the Coronation of George II in 1727. The same anthem has been used since before the Norman Conquest. Our coronation ceremonial therefore has links with attitudes and traditions which go back several thousand years.

Much of the ritual and significance of the Coronation is not religious of course. For example the crown itself is probably derived from the distinctive helmet which the leader of the tribe or group would have worn in battle. The style of the robes with which the monarch is invested during the course of the coronation ceremonial is based on ecclesiastical robes, but these vestments probably also carry a reminder of a pre-Christian rite, when the new king was clothed in the armour of the old to show clearly that he took on both the responsibilities and the rights of his predecessor. The use of a throne to elevate the new Sovereign so that he is clearly visible to the people, and to impress on them his exalted state, may well be based on the custom of carrying a newly triumphant chieftain on the shields of his peers. Finally the presentation of military equipment, swords and spurs, although it is adapted to Christian significance in the

James II being crowned in Westminster Abbey, 1685

Coronation, quite clearly has a perfectly practical origin which owes little to religion.

The use of a Christian religious ceremony to uphold temporal power was first evident in Europe in the middle of the eighth century, when Pippin was anointed by the church in order to ensure that his claim to be next ruler of the Franks was not disputed. Pippin's son, the Emperor Charlemagne, repeated the process, and so gave it greater force, when he had his own sons anointed by Pope Hadrian I in Rome. As a result, the Christian Church began to play a powerful part in deciding who had the right to rule.

It was probably as a result of the example of such a powerful ruler as Charlemagne that in 787 the Anglo-Saxon king of Mercia, Offa, had his own son, Ecgfrith, anointed with oil to dispel any doubts about his succession. The first true English Coronation Service is generally acknowledged to be that of King Edgar at Bath Abbey on Whit Sunday 973. This service was remarkably similar to the most recent Coronation in 1953. Edgar made a Promise which corresponds to the modern Coronation Oath, using the words:

These three things I promise in Christ's name to the Christian People subject to me: First, that the Church of God and the whole Christian People shall have true peace at all time by our judgement; Second, that I will forbid extortion and all kinds of wrong-doing to all orders of men; Third, that I will enjoin equity and mercy in all judgements, that God, Who is kind and merciful, may vouchsafe His mercy to me and to you.

Before he could make that promise, Edgar had to be formally elected by the people. Nowadays the Sovereign similarly has to be 'Recognized' by the people in the Abbey before the ceremony can continue. Edgar was anointed by the Bishop just as Elizabeth II was, while the anthem sung was 'Zadok the Priest' just as it was 1,000 years later. He was invested with the outward symbols of his authority and power, a sword and a ring; so too, in a more elaborate ceremonial, was Elizabeth II. Edgar was crowned, an act which nowadays seems the most significant part of the ceremonial to many people, and like his successor 1,000 years later he was placed on a throne set above the rest of the congregation, so that his people could do him homage. Then as now, the entire rite was incorporated into a religious service. In the tenth century it was a mass, now it is a Protestant Communion Service.

The Coronation Service which was used in 973, and which still forms the basis of the Coronation Service of the twentieth century with its five elements of Recognition, Oath, Anointing, Investiture and Homage, was devised by St Dunstan, who was Archbishop of Canterbury. It was clearly based on similar coronation ceremonies being evolved in other countries of Christian Europe, and it emphasized the inter-relationship between the Sovereign, the People, and the Church, all of whom derived what rights they had from God. So the Coronation Service which in some ways has changed remarkably little since it was first used, emphasizes the

A page from the fourteenth-century *Liber Regalis* showing the crowning of a monarch

unity of all the component parts of the nation under God and gives that unity added prestige by underlining its long historical precedent.

In the fourteenth century the form of the Coronation Service was substantially overhauled to take account of changing circumstances and the ever-fluctuating changes in the balance of power between the Sovereign, the Church, and the People. The new order was first used for the Coronation of the boy king Richard II in 1377 and is embodied in an illuminated manuscript called the *Liber Regalis* (*The Royal Book*) which is still in the library at Westminster Abbey.

Westminster Abbey was built by King Edward, later known as St Edward the Confessor, specifically with the idea of its being used for coronations. For this reason it was designed with a very wide central area known as the 'Theatre' where the Sovereign is presented for formal Recognition. When Henry III rebuilt the Abbey he preserved the Theatre so that Westminster Abbey as it is today is clearly the Coronation Church which Edward the Confessor had intended. Until the Abbey was built English kings were crowned in any city which was convenient. St Edward the Confessor himself was crowned in 1043 at Winchester, which was a popular choice. In some cases kings were crowned in more than one town to make sure there was no doubt in the minds of the people who was right-ful ruler. This is not as unnecessary as it first sounds, when it is considered how poor communications were such a long time ago.

The first king to be crowned in Westminster Abbey was the ill-fated Harold, who was defeated shortly after at the battle of Hastings in 1066. Not surprisingly William the Conqueror chose to be crowned in the Abbey to emphasize his own legality and continuity with his predecessors. Since then the only monarchs not to be crowned in the Abbey were Edward V – one of the little princes who died in the Tower – and Edward VIII whose relationship with Mrs Simpson led to his abdication before he was crowned.

The venerable Abbey has adapted remarkably well to the demands of a modern spectacle – the need to accommodate some 7,000 people and to film and televise the entire ceremony. Until the coronation of Edward VII in 1911 there had not even been any photographs of the ceremony; photo-graphy was in its infancy when Queen Victoria was crowned in 1838.

The first Coronation to be filmed was that of the Queen's father, George VI in 1937. The Coronation of Elizabeth II in 1953 was the first time the ceremony was both filmed and televised. The use of the new medium, television, enabled millions of people to see a ceremony which previously had been witnessed only by hundreds. Indeed many people's first memory of watching television is of sitting round one of the tiny screens with all their neighbours watching the Coronation and the televising of the ceremony boosted the sales of television sets enormously. However, it did place an added strain on the participants, and in particular the Queen, which had never been experienced by their predecessors. The demands for perfection in both performance and timing put the 1953 Coronation in a league apart from any other and revealed how much the monarchy had become a public relations exercise. The little mishaps of the past, which in many ways had contributed to the individuality and interest of the event, could not be allowed to happen. The Earl Marshal of England, the Duke of Norfolk, whose job it was to co-ordinate, meticulously plan, and rehearse the entire operation would have shuddered at an incident such as that during the Coronation in 1830 of 'Sailor' King William IV who, when asked for his oblation (his gift to the Church) answered in his own straightforward, naval fashion, 'I do not have anything. I will send it to you tomorrow.'

CORONATION OF HER MAJESTY
QUEEN ELIZABETH II

By Command of The Queen

the Earl Marshal is directed to invite

to be present at the Abbey Church of
Westminster on the 2nd day of June 1953

Norfolk.
Earl Marshal

An invitation to the Coronation of Elizabeth II, signed by the Duke of Norfolk, Earl Marshal. Joan Hassall's design incorporates the Royal Coat of Arms, part of the Regalia and flowers (or plants) associated with each of the Commonwealth countries

At the 1838 Coronation of Queen Victoria, the ring, which had been measured for her little finger, was pushed onto her larger fourth finger with brute force by the Archbishop of Canterbury ('as usual *so* confused and puzzled' she wrote later in her diary) so that 'the consequence was that I had the greatest difficulty to take it off again, which I did at last with great pain'. More amusingly at the same Coronation, as Victoria recalls, the eighty-two-year-old peer Lord Rolle, missed his footing while going to do homage and rolled down the steps.

However, it is a great pity that the spectacular Coronation of George IV in 1821 could not be committed to film. While he was Prince Regent George's extravagances had shocked the country and caused him to fall out with his father, George III. Like Edward VII he had waited a long time for his turn to be king – he was sixty when at last he was crowned – and his Coronation and Coronation Banquet (a custom which was afterwards dis-

17

continued because George's conspicuous consumption caused so much offence) were the epitome of costly vulgarity. In all it required a grant from Parliament of nearly a quarter of a million pounds, worth a great deal, more, of course, in modern money. The King, who as a young man had been handsome and stylish, had become bloated and over-dressed. Harriet Arbuthnot, the wife of the MP Charles Arbuthnot, while appalled at the King himself, 'The King behaved very indecently; he was continually nodding and winking at Lady Conyngham' (his mistress), could not help being moved by the ceremony and the loyal demonstrations of the crowd:

It is not possible to describe anything finer than the scene was, the galleries all standing up waving their hats and handkerchiefs and shouting, 'God Bless the King!' Altogether it was a scene I would not have missed seeing for the world, and shall never see again so fine a one.

Because George's successor, his brother William IV, was more spartan in his attitudes and his habits, his own Coronation was a total contrast. In deciding to dispense with the banquet which had been an integral part of the coronation pageantry since the time of the Conqueror, William also brought to an end several quaintly colourful customs which were associated with it. The first of these was the idea of the monarch dining in public as a public show. In medieval times this had been a part of everyday life for the king or queen. But gradually it was dispensed with as many monarchs, such as Elizabeth I, found it irksome. The Coronation Banquet was the last surviving instance of the old custom. After the coronation ceremonial the monarch and his peers would process back to Westminster Hall to eat a vast banquet watched by spectators in the gallery. It was quite usual for those taking part in the feast to send food to their friends and relatives

The Coronation Procession of Charles II, 1661. Painting by Dirck Stoop

who lowered baskets down for the purpose. Anything remaining was then left to the public. De Saussurce, a contemporary Frenchman, wrote of the Banquet following George II's Coronation:

The pillage was most diverting; the people threw themselves with astonishing avidity on everything the hall contained; blows were given and returned, and I cannot give you any idea of the noise and confusion that reigned. In less than half an hour everything had disappeared, even the boards of which the tables and seats had been made.

Before the Coronation the King and peers used to assemble in Westminster Hall before processing to the Abbey. Ahead of them went the King's herbwoman and six garlanded young girls who scattered flowers and sweet smelling herbs in their path. It was not only a graceful gesture but for many years had been considered a way of warding off the plague as well as counteracting the smell of the crowds. This attractive piece of minor ceremonial was abandoned after George IV's Coronation when the use of Westminster Hall was abandoned. So too was the custom of the King having a canopy held over his head during the walk from Westminster Hall to the Abbey. It had been the privilege of the Barons of the Cinque Ports (Dover, Hastings, Rye, Romney, Hythe, Sandwich, and Winchelsea) to carry this canopy. In subsequent Coronations they were given other ceremonial duties to compensate for the loss of the honour.

The most spectacular ceremony which William IV's very admirable economy brought an end to was the formal Challenge by the King's Champion, who rode into the banquet on a charger, wearing full armour and accompanied by the Lord High Constable and the Earl Marshal of England, both in their coronation robes and coronets. In front of them walked Garter King of Arms, carrying a scroll on which was written the Challenge.

It was the privilege of the Cinque Port Barons to carry the canopy, shown here held over Mary of Modena, wife of James II, in his Coronation Procession, 1685

Two esquires carried the challenger's shield and lance and trumpeters punctuated each stage of the Challenge with a loud fanfare.

Garter King of Arms read out the Challenge which was as follows:

If any person of what degree soever, high or low, shall deny or gainsay, Our Sovereign Lord King, King of England, France and Ireland, Duke of Normandy and Acquitaine, next heir to Sovereign Lord King. . . . the Last King deceased, to be Heir to the Imperial Crown of this Realm of England, or that he ought not to enjoy the same, Here is his Champion, who sayeth that he lyeth, and is a False Traytor, being ready in Person to Combat with him; and in this Quarrel will adventure his life against him, on what day soever shall be appointed.

The King's Champion rides into George IV's Coronation Banquet (1820) accompanied by the Lord High Chancellor and the Earl Marshal

The King's Champion then threw down his gauntlet, which was picked up after a few minutes by one of the heralds when it was obvious that no one was going to respond. Twice more the gauntlet was thrown down with all due ceremony and twice more the herald retrieved it. By this stage the procession had reached the dais. The King then rose to his feet and ceremonially drank the health of his Champion after which he presented him with the gilt cup and cover from which the toast had been drunk. Having drunk the King's health from the same cup the Champion retained it as a reward for his service and rode with his escort out of the hall. This required the ability to ride a horse backwards out of the King's presence, no mean feat in itself.

The King's Champion since the reign of Edward II at the beginning of the fourteenth century, was always a member of the Dymoke family, Lords of the Manor of Scrivelsby in Lincolnshire. Many other duties of the Coronation were also hereditary, associated with the ownership of certain areas of land or with particular offices. Not all of these duties have become obsolete like that of the King's Champion. Many, such as carrying the gold spurs or the Royal Standard of Scotland, are still part of the ceremonial in the Abbey. Although the material rewards of such service are no longer available, for many people the honour involved is valued even more highly. Those who think for any reason that they are entitled to perform one of the services have to submit their claims to the Court of Claims. Nowadays the Court of Claims is a Commission of the Privy Council, but its origins go back to the fourteenth century when a Court sat before the Coronation of Richard II to sort out the conflicting claims of those seeking to secure the ceremonial duties and the financial rewards which went with them. Interestingly, even before the most recent Coronation of Elizabeth II the ceremonial duties were not all straightforward. A Court of Claims had to be set up and many claims, some of them more ludicrous than others, needed to be resolved.

THE CORONATION SERVICE

The twentieth-century Coronation of Elizabeth II was based on the fourteenth-century *Liber Regalis* although inevitably there have been modifications over the centuries. Basically the order as laid down by the *Liber Regalis* can be reduced to five clear sequences: the Recognition, the Oath, the Anointing, the Investiture, and the Homage.

Before the ceremony started formal processions of the most important guests had to arrive and be seated. The first of these processions was the Lord Mayor's Procession. Next came a procession of foreign dignitaries. Third came the Prime Minister's Procession which included the Prime Ministers and representatives of Commonwealth countries and overseas territories. Last came the Royal Procession which culminated in the Queen's own Procession. The duty of some of the participants was to carry items of the Coronation Regalia which had been brought from the Tower of London the day before and kept overnight in the Jerusalem Chamber guarded by the Yeomen of the Guard.

The Commonwealth Standards at the Coronation of George V, 1910. From left to right: South Africa, Australia, New Zealand and Canada

The Queen's Procession itself formed up in a specially built annexe by the Abbey, where the various items of regalia were distributed to those who had been accorded the privilege of carrying them. When the Procession reached the centre of the Abbey, the 'Theatre', where a platform approached by steps from all sides had been built, the Queen took a few moments for private prayer while the Regalia were placed upon the altar. The Queen then went to the throne in the centre of the dais for the *Recognition*. She turned to show herself to all four sides of the Abbey as the Archbishop of Canterbury went to the east, south, west, and north of the Theatre and at each spoke the following words:

'Sirs, I here present unto you Queen Elizabeth, your undoubted Queen: Wherefore all you who are come this day to do your homage and service, Are you willing to do the same?'

To this at each time the people signified 'their willingness and joy' by crying out 'God Save Queen Elizabeth'; after which the trumpets sounded a fanfare.

Next came the *Oath*. In 1953 Elizabeth II swore to govern the people of the United Kingdom and of her territories abroad according to their laws and customs. She also vowed to uphold law and justice tempered with mercy and to maintain the established Protestant Church. With her hand on the Bible she swore 'The things which I have here before promised I will perform and keep. So help me God.' The Moderator of the Church of

Scotland then presented her with a Bible with the words 'Here is Wisdom; This is the royal Law; These are the lively Oracles of God.'

The next in the sequence is the *Anointing*, from the religious point of view the most important part of the entire ceremony. At this stage, therefore, began the Communion service into which the coronation ceremonial is integrated. After prayers the Queen was divested of the crimson robe she was wearing and in a simple white gown which symbolized her humility in the face of God she was escorted to King Edward's Chair, which has been used as the Coronation Chair for over six hundred years. It was made by Edward I to house the 'Stone of Scone', which he captured from the Scots in 1296 and which, on several occasions, they have tried to win back. As she sat there, four Knights of the Garter held a rich silken canopy over her.

A little oil was poured from the Ampulla, a golden vessel in the form of an eagle to symbolize imperial power, into the Anointing Spoon which dates from the twelfth century. The Archbishop of Canterbury then anointed the Queen three times saying '. . . be thou anointed, blessed, and consecrated, Queen over the Peoples, whom the Lord thy God hath given thee to rule and govern.'

After the Anointing the Queen retired to St Edward's Chapel, where she put on a white tunic and the rich golden robe (*supertunica*) of a Sovereign Queen in preparation for her Investment with the outward signs of her worldly power. Although the *Investiture* is a sign of her temporal as opposed to her spiritual strength the items of the Regalia do all have a religious symbolism as well.

First she touched the Gold Spurs, which were then laid on the altar; the spurs symbolized her adherence to the code of chivalry and had she been a man they would have been attached to her heels, or, as in the case of George v and v I, they would have touched his heels. The Sword of State and the Jewelled Sword which were next dedicated to God are symbolic of the Sovereign's intention to punish evil-doers. Three other swords are carried during the Coronation although they are not used during the Investiture. These are a blunt sword (the Curtana) which symbolizes mercy, the Sword of Spiritual Justice, and the Sword of Temporal Justice.

Next the Archbishop fastened on the Queen's wrists the Armills, 'bracelets of sincerity and wisdom', which symbolize God's protection and the bond which unites the Sovereign with the people. After this the Stole and Robe Royal were put on and the Queen was given the Orb surmounted by a cross, to show 'the whole world is subject to the Power and Empire of Christ our Redeemer'. This was then laid on the altar. The Ring, a sapphire and ruby cross set in gold, denoting the 'wedding' of Sovereign and people, was placed on the fourth finger of the Queen's right hand. A Glove was then put on and the Sceptre with the Cross, 'the ensign of kingly power and justice', was placed in the monarch's right hand. In the left hand was held the Sceptre with the Dove which signifies justice and mercy.

The climax of the Investiture is the crowning. The congregation rose as the Archbishop took St Edward's Crown from the altar and placed it 'reverently' upon the Sovereign's head. At this a great shout of 'God Save the Queen' went up. The princes and princesses, peers and peeresses put on their coronets and caps and the Kings of Arms their crowns. The trumpets sounded and simultaneously a salute of guns was fired on Tower Hill. Queen Victoria wrote of the same moment at her own Coronation, 'The shouts, which were very great, the drums, the trumpets, the firing of the guns, all at the same instant, rendered the spectacle most imposing.'

The Regalia. Top, from left to right: King Edward's Crown, Orb, Coronation Ring, Crown of State. Bottom, from left to right: Sword of Mercy, Sword of Justice, Sword of Spiritual Justice, King Edward's Chair, Sceptre with Dove, St Edward's Staff, Sceptre with Cross

The Queen then returned to the throne in the centre of the Theatre where, invested with all the symbols of worldly power, she received the homage of the people. Because St Edward's Crown is incredibly heavy, it is actually written into the Order of the Coronation that the Bishops of Durham and Bath and Wells who support the Sovereign may help to take the weight of the Crown during the *Homage*.

First the Archbishop of Canterbury did Homage on behalf of the Bishops. Next, her Consort, Prince Philip, did his Homage, and after him the Royal Dukes. The Senior Peer of each degree then did Homage on behalf of the others. The wording used in 1953 differed little from the wording used in medieval times. So the Queen's husband having removed his coronet pledged his loyalty with the ancient words:

I, Philip, Duke of Edinburgh, do become your liege man of life and limb, and of earthly worship; and faith and truth I will bear unto you, to live and die, against all manner of folks. So help me God.

After doing Homage, each peer who represented his rank touched the Crown to symbolize his support for the wearer and kissed the Queen on the left cheek if he were a Royal Duke, otherwise on the right hand. After the Homage and before the Communion service resumed the drums beat and the trumpets sounded yet again while the people cried out 'God Save Queen Elizabeth. Long Live Queen Elizabeth. May the Queen Live Forever.'

Elizabeth II receiving the kiss of homage from her husband, Prince Philip, Duke of Edinburgh, at her Coronation, 1953

As is the custom the Queen offered a gift, an 'oblation' to the Church, before the Communion service began. At the end of the Communion the *Te Deum* was sung while the Queen went into St Edward's Chapel to be divested of the Royal Robe, St Edward's Crown, and the Sceptre with the Dove. She put on a robe of purple velvet and exchanged St Edward's

The Queen returning to
Buckingham Palace in the
Great State Coach after her
Coronation

Crown for the lighter Imperial State Crown. Holding the Orb and the
Sceptre with the Cross she then processed out of the Abbey and continued
her Procession in the Great State Coach back to Buckingham Palace.
Unlike the short walk of many previous monarchs between the Abbey
and Westminster Hall the Queen took a circuitous route which lengthened
the journey between Westminster and Buckingham Palace to five miles.
It allowed many thousands who had waited in the rain to get a glimpse of
her and to cheer their newly crowned Sovereign. It rounded off a Coronation
ceremony which in every way had been more carefully planned with the
awareness of those watching, in person and on television, than any other
Coronation before. As such it foreshadowed the whole tone of the rest of
the Queen's reign for she, more than any of her predecessors, has shown an
understanding of the importance of publicity and of the role of the monarch
as a symbol and focus of the unity of millions of people.

CORONATION OF SOVEREIGN'S CONSORT

When Elizabeth II was crowned her husband was not crowned with her.
In Britain it has never been the custom for the husbands of queens regnant
to be crowned king. This stems from a quite understandable fear that such
a 'king', in the days when women were regarded as subject to their husbands and monarchs wielded real power, would assume his own superiority
over his wife and take over her supreme position. Since royal princesses
tended to marry foreign princes to cement alliances with countries abroad
the danger of a foreign prince becoming an unwanted king was considered

too great. Elizabeth I solved the problem by not marrying at all. Mary II's husband, William III, was crowned as equal monarch with her by virtue of the fact that by overthrowing her father, James II, he had virtually conquered the country and his position as the overthrown James II's son-in-law was in some senses nothing more than a piece of elaborate window-dressing. Both Mary Tudor in the sixteenth century and Queen Victoria three hundred years later were so besotted by their husbands that they attempted to change the usual procedure and have them accepted as king, but each time the force of public opinion quickly scotched the idea. When Elizabeth II came to the throne in 1952 the idea was not even mooted. However, the wives of kings are always crowned as their status is considered to be derived from their husbands. Only George IV, who loathed his promiscuous wife Caroline of Brunswick, refused to allow her to participate in the Coronation and when she arrived uninvited at the door of Westminster Abbey she was unceremoniously turned away, to the delight of the crowds who were waiting outside for a glimpse of the Procession. Henry VIII, perhaps becoming blasé, did not bother to go through with the ceremony for his last four wives, although Anne Boleyn did at least have the satisfaction of a Coronation to compensate for her beheading less than three years later!

Anne set out for Westminster from the Tower where the night before Henry VIII had created eighteen new Knights of the Bath which was the custom before the coronation of a king or queen regnant. Cranmer, who actually crowned her, describes the ceremony:

And so her Grace sustained of each side with two bishops, . . . came forth in procession unto the Church of Westminster, she in her hair, my Lord Suffolk bearing before her the Crown, and two other Lords bearing also before her a sceptre and a white rod, and so entered up into the High Altar, where divers ceremonies used about her, I did set the crown on her head, and then was sung Te Deum etc.

In two cases it was the queens themselves who refused to be crowned. Both Henrietta Maria, wife of Charles I, and Catherine of Braganza, who married Charles II, were Roman Catholics. Since the Coronation is basically a religious service which makes a feature of the monarch's duty to uphold the Protestant religion, they declined on religious grounds. They may also have underestimated the significance of the event for only in England are queens consort crowned, the precedent having been set by Eleanor, wife of Henry II, who was crowned with him in 1154. If the king marries after his own Coronation then the queen consort may be crowned in a separate ceremony later.

The queen consort is both anointed and crowned after the peers have done their homage to the king. First she is anointed on the head and breast. She is then invested with a purple robe. Next she is crowned with a special crown which is usually made for that purpose only and broken up again after the queen's death. A ring is put on the fourth finger of the queen's right hand and she receives a sceptre and a rod. Next, supported by two bishops, the newly crowned queen is taken to her throne in the Theatre of the Abbey. This throne is placed slightly lower than that of the king and as she passes his throne she makes an obeisance. The coronation ceremony then continues as usual with the Communion service.

As already mentioned the Coronation of Elizabeth II on 2 June 1953 was more meticulously organized than any other. Future coronations can be expected to follow an almost identical pattern, allowing for inevitable changes in national and world politics.

Place **Westminster Abbey**
Route to the Abbey **The Procession from Buckingham Palace took the following route: The Mall – Admiralty Arch – Trafalgar Square – Northumberland Avenue – Victoria Embankment – Parliament Square – Westminster Abbey.**
Route from the Abbey **was via Parliament Square – Whitehall – Trafalgar Square – Pall Mall – St James's Street – Piccadilly – East Carriage Drive – Oxford Street – Oxford Circus – Regent Street – Piccadilly Circus – Haymarket – Trafalgar Square – The Mall – Buckingham Palace.**
Times **By 8.30 a.m. the route was lined with troops and from then onwards a number of various Processions made their way to the Abbey. These left in the following order and at the following times:**
8.40 a.m. The Lord Mayor of London's Procession. The Speaker of the House of Commons. Motor Cavalcade of certain members of the Royal Family and Representatives of Foreign Powers.
9.15 a.m. Carriage Procession of Prime Ministers, Representatives of India and Burma and Colonial Rulers.
9.49 a.m. Carriage Procession of the Royal Family.
10.13 a.m. Carriage Procession of Queen Mother.
10.30 a.m. Sovereign left Buckingham Palace.
11.00 a.m. Sovereign arrived at Westminster Abbey.
1.45 p.m. End of Coronation Service.
2.15 p.m. Prime Ministers, Colonial Rulers, Royal Family, etc. left Westminster Abbey.
2.45 p.m. Sovereign's Procession left Westminster Abbey.
4.30 p.m. Sovereign's Procession returned to Buckingham Palace.
5.20 p.m. Sovereign and Royal Family appeared on balcony, R.A.F. fly-past.
  On the return journey it took the Sovereign one hour forty minutes to travel the 5 miles 250 yards to the Palace. The two-mile procession took forty-five minutes to pass any point.
Full details of route and times are given in the Press.

Members of the public are allowed to line the route from the Palace to the Abbey but the area around the Abbey is kept clear and even those at the closest points are likely to have their views marred by rows of guardsmen. Back at the Palace, people may gather round the Victoria Memorial, and along the Mall, but nobody is allowed to stand near the Palace railings. Only when the Sovereign has returned to the Palace may the crowds approach the railings to witness the balcony appearance and fly-past.

At past coronations literally hundreds of thousands of people have thronged to each and every vantage point along the whole route of the procession. Many have taken up their positions as early as two or three days before the event, fully equipped for a long stay.

To get a position along the route you need to arrive at least the night before or in the early hours of the morning. At the last Coronation in 1953 stands were placed along key positions of the route and around the Abbey, in which seats could cost as much as £50 each. Balconies along the route cost £3,500 for 50 people, including champagne. If you allow for over 30 years' inflation, the next Coronation will be very costly for those who wish to guarantee their view! Seats in the Abbey are obviously very limited and strictly by invitation only. Those invited include members of the Royal Family, dignitaries from all over the world, important public figures, and a number of people who have given great service to the community.

The State Opening of Parliament

The State Opening of Parliament is the annual ceremony which best sums up the role of constitutional monarchy in Britain. It reveals the limitations of its power while emphasizing the importance of its role as the figurehead of government. The pomp and pageantry which surround the occasion remind us yet again of the practical importance of much of our royal ceremonial, for it is by being scrupulous in the preservation of the outward forms of our democracy that we can be more certain of preserving the reality underneath.

British Parliamentary democracy does not have a constitution drawn up and imposed on it overnight. It has been evolving and adapting to circumstances since the times of the pre-Conquest Saxon kings. Its origins are very simple. The king was one among his peers (his equals) who, usually through outstanding abilities of leadership, sometimes combined with inheritance, was elected as leader. Naturally his peers, while accepting leadership, wished to have their points of view taken into consideration as well. It was therefore customary for the king to listen to the advice of all, or a chosen few, among his peers. These constituted his council, and today the Queen has a Privy (private) Council which is supposed to fulfil the same function as the councils of ancient kings.

William the Conqueror adapted the existing Saxon customs of government to his own use and combined them with his own Norman customs. In practice this meant that two or three times a year he called to his court a group of barons whom he would consult. They were still technically his peers but they were mindful of the fact that they owed their lands and rank to the king's good will and their position was inevitably a subservient one. The Church too, because it maintained that kings held their position by the Grace of God as demonstrated through the anointing by a bishop, and because many of the clergy were rich landowners as well, also expected to be listened to at these councils. The common people, those without titles, were not consulted at all.

During the Middle Ages the term Parliament came to be used for these councils. This word derived from the Norman French word for talk, since that is what the meetings were all about. At the same time government, as it always tends to do, began to get heavy with bureaucracy, so that Parliament was usually held at the king's palace of Westminster, rather than following him on his progress round the various towns and cities of the kingdom.

The signing of Magna Carta in 1215, which put some of the people's customary rights down on paper, and the rebellion of Simon de Montfort in the 1260s in demand of greater rights of consultation with the king, are often cited as the first signs of democracy as we recognize it today. Although they undoubtedly helped to curtail the theoretically boundless power of the monarch a little, they did not greatly increase the privilege of the 'commons', the majority of people, without title, land or wealth.

Further encroachment of the king's power over the next 200 years came less through rebellion than through the fact that the king needed money and he was not able to collect taxes from the people without first having the consent of Parliament. So it became possible to blackmail the king to accord certain privileges in return for raising taxes. The king's need for taxes was also the reason for the infiltration of the 'commons' into Parliament, for often it was not the aristocracy which could provide the money but people made rich through trade and commerce. To this day we are reminded of one of the sources of the country's and therefore the king's wealth at this period in one of the customs of the House of Lords. The Chancellor sits before the throne on the Woolsack as a reminder of what was once the major source of the wealth of the realm.

Henry VIII allowed a further encroachment of monarchical power in the sixteenth century when he brought about the Protestant Reformation in England. By this time, because of the necessity of raising money for government from a wider section of the community, Parliament consisted

The House of Commons
presenting the Speaker to
Elizabeth I at Westminster

30

31

of two groups. These were the peers, who claimed a hereditary right to be consulted by a king who, in theory at least, was one of their number, and the commons from whom much of the real money came. However, the commons was a group of distinguished and privileged people: it was not the all-embracing group we would understand by the term today but rather a group of rich people who did not have titles. Both peers and commons wrung more privileges from Henry VIII in return for enacting the legislation he required to oust the power of the Catholic Church and replace it with a more manageable English one.

The Civil War of 1642-48 is the next obvious stage in the development of Parliament towards a broader based democracy. The Stuart kings believed in a notion which was foreign to most Englishmen, peers and commons alike, that the king was not first among equals but created superior by God and invested by him, rather than by the people, with his power. Because of their belief in their divine origins the Stuarts believed that their power should not be questioned, and because it was invested in them alone it should not be subject to any interference from their subjects whatever their rank. For eleven years Charles I ruled by himself and refused to consult Parliament. In 1641 John Pym, a member of the House of Commons, demanded a restitution and increase of the rights of Parliament as set out in his Grand Remonstrance. Charles I refused to comply: it made no sense to him to do so with his notion of the Divine Right of Kings. He then committed the cardinal sin of marching uninvited into the chamber of the House of Commons, where, as a member of the aristocracy, he had no right to go, and tried to arrest the five most prominent men there. They had already fled to the City of London, a power centre of immensely wealthy commoners, and Charles I by marching into the City with an army antagonized them further. In addition his theories of kingship did not accord with the beliefs of many of the House of Lords, although in romantic fiction the war between King and Parliament is always portrayed as a war between Parliament and Aristocracy. It is not surprising therefore that despite many initial advantages the King, who had antagonized so many section of society, was eventually the loser and was beheaded. Ironically the rule of Oliver Cromwell was in some ways as much of a dictatorship as that of the Stuart kings. When Charles II was restored to the throne in 1660, after Cromwell's death, it was because of the belief of most people that he would be more willing to recognize the demands of Parliament, and in particular the House of Commons, to play its part in the government of the country. The concessions which Charles II made in order to recover his throne were a major step towards the type of democracy we have today. It was in his reign that the two-party system which we are accustomed to began to evolve.

The Civil War was the last major civil upheaval in Britain. The further erosion of the power of the monarch and of his peers in the House of Lords, an erosion which has reflected the altered balance of power in the country, has been a gradual and fundamentally peaceful process.

It was during Queen Victoria's reign that the constitutional monarchy we accept as our system of government today became recognizable. This was partly due to the influence over the Queen of Prince Albert, who saw that the society which had undergone the industrial revolution needed a sovereign who could accept the new order and adapt herself to a different but still useful role. During Victoria's reign the number of people entitled to vote was greatly increased so that the eventual total enfranchisement of all men and women over the age of twenty-one after the First World War was set on an inevitable course. Prince Albert also saw the values of the ceremonial function of monarchy as a means of uniting people by reminding them of their joint past and exploiting the emotions which great occasions usually evoke.

Today the real power of Queen Elizabeth is very curtailed, although it is still her responsibility to call on a leader of one of the parties to form a government. In moments of national crisis when the candidate is not obvious, that choice could be vital. In theory the function of government is carried out in her name, so that whatever the underlying conflicts between different factions and parties the nation presents a united front in the person of its impartial Head of State and her Government which is responsible to her. So when the Queen opens Parliament in October or November each year, she reads a speech from the throne in the House of Lords in which she speaks of the proposals of 'my government' for the coming year. But everyone knows the speech has been written for her by that government and she cannot in practice question its proposals. In the same way she gives her assent to legislation. Without this Acts of Parliament cannot become law, but in practice the Queen would never withhold her assent from a properly legislated Act of Parliament presented to her by a legitimate government. This apparent charade is connived at by intelligent people because it is felt that the Queen's necessary involvement provides a system which makes it harder for abuses to creep in. Similarly, justice is considered to have its fount in the Crown, which is totally impartial, and therefore gives justice greater credibility.

One additional factor, which was true of the first really constitutional monarch, Queen Victoria, and is true of Elizabeth ii who has reigned for thirty years, is that a Head of State who holds the position for life becomes a unique source of experience and knowledge which changing governments can consult to their advantage.

The ceremonial of the State Opening of Parliament carries many reminders of the hundreds of years of history which have resulted in the type of parliament we have today. One feature is the ritual searching of

Yeomen of the Guard
carrying lanterns, going to
search the cellars of the
Houses of Parliament before
its State Opening

the cellars of the Houses of Parliament by a detachment of the Yeomen of
the Guard carrying lanterns. Although Parliament is now housed in a
building designed and built in the nineteenth century in the medieval style,
and the cellars are not those where the original incident took place, this
search is a result of the Gunpowder Plot. On 5 November 1605 Yeoman of
the Guard, warned that a plot was being hatched, searched the cellars of
the Houses of Parliament and found Guy Fawkes on the point of blowing
the building up with a large quantity of gunpowder. Together with his
co-conspirators he plotted against James I whose policies had alienated a
section of the nobility. Since then the search by the Yeomen has taken
place before every State Opening. More recently its ceremonial aspect has
been rather overshadowed by the need for such searches in earnest because
of the constant shadow of terrorism, and the Yeomen have been joined by
police and army experts.

On the day of the State Opening the Queen drives from Buckingham
Palace in the Irish State Coach to reach the Houses of Parliament by
11.00 a.m. This procession is a stirring sight. The Sovereign is escorted
by the Household Cavalry whose magnificent horses, shining armour, and
distinctive plumed helmets add star quality to any ceremonial occasion.
The route is lined with guardsmen and a Guard of Honour is waiting to
greet the Queen on her arrival. There is music from a military band which
strikes up the National Anthem as the Queen approaches. One of the most
fascinating parts of the procession is the Royal Regalia; the Imperial State
Crown, the Cap of Maintenance, the Sword of State, and the maces of the

Serjeants-at-Arms. These items are brought to Buckingham Palace from their permanent home in the Tower of London the night before the State Opening. In the morning they precede the Sovereign in the procession in their own coach, Queen Alexandra's State Coach. They are entitled to the compliment of an Escort of Troopers of the Household Cavalry and are saluted by the troops along the route. The Regalia Escort itself pays only one compliment – it salutes the Cenotaph as it passes down Whitehall. Displayed in this way the Regalia are a clear reminder of the Sovereign's authority. The crown which the Sovereign wears to open Parliament is the Imperial State Crown, which was made for Queen Victoria's Coronation in 1838. It is used because it is considerably lighter than St Edward's Crown, although it weighs some three pounds. It incorporates some historic jewels, including the Black Prince's ruby which was worn by Henry v at Agincourt, a sapphire reputed to have come from Edward the Confessor's ring, and pearls which belonged to Elizabeth i. The costly magnificence of the crown with its 3,000 jewels symbolizes the majesty of the Sovereign. George v, a stickler for doing everything quite correctly, reverted to wearing the crown with its clear symbolism, rather than the military cocked-hat favoured by Edward vii. Nevertheless he conceded that there could be a few ordeals worse than being obliged to deliver someone else's speech while balancing the crown on his head. Of the rest of the Regalia, the velvet Cap of Maintenance signifies the Queen's religious orthodoxy, the jewelled Sword of State indicates her intention to defend justice. Once the Queen is seated in Parliament one specially chosen peer will stand on her right holding the Cap, while another will stand on her left holding the Sword of State. The Regalia are again displayed in their lighted coach on the return journey to the Palace, when they follow the Queen's coach.

At the Sovereign's entrance of the Houses of Parliament, the Queen is greeted by the Earl Marshal of England and the Lord Great Chamberlain who is hereditary Keeper of the Royal Palace of Westminster. A fanfare of trumpets is sounded and they walk backwards before the Queen as she enters. They and the heralds then escort her up the staircase, which is guarded by dismounted cavalry holding swords, to the Robing Room. There the Queen puts on the Imperial State Crown and the Crimson Robe of State which was made for Queen Victoria. This robe has a train some eighteen feet long, which is carried by four pages in scarlet and yellow livery.

The Procession which is to enter the House of Lords forms up in the Royal Gallery where there is room for members of the public to view the proceedings. When the Queen is ready the doors are opened to a fanfare of trumpets and she joins the Procession, her left hand resting on the right hand of the Duke of Edinburgh who escorts her. The people who make up

The Queen's Procession in
the House of Lords at the
State Opening of Parliament. The Queen and
Prince Philip are preceded
by the Cap of State and
the Sword of State, borne
by peers

this Procession are listed in their correct order in 'Ceremonial to be Observed
at the Opening of Parliament by Her Majesty the Queen'. It is as follows:

Fitzalan Pursuivant Extraordinary	Rouge Dragon Pursuivant
Rouge Croix Pursuivant	Portcullis Pursuivant
Wales Herald Extraordinary	Norfolk Herald Extraordinary
Arundel Herald Extraordinary	Lancaster Herald
York Herald	Somerset Herald
Richmond Herald	Windsor Herald

Gentleman Usher to Her Majesty	Private Secretary to HRH The Prince Philip Duke of Edinburgh	Gentleman Usher to Her Majesty
Serjeant-at-Arms		Serjeant-at-Arms
Equerry in Waiting to Her Majesty	The Crown Equerry	Equerry in Waiting to Her Majesty
The Comptroller of Her Majesty's Household		The Treasurer of Her Majesty's Household

The Keeper of Her Majesty's Privy Purse	The Private Secretary to Her Majesty	
Norroy and Ulster King of Arms	Clarenceux King of Arms	
The Lord Privy Seal	The Lord President of the Council	

The Lord High
Chancellor

The Gentleman Usher of the Black Rod	Garter King of Arms
The Earl Marshal	The Lord Great Chamberlain
The Sword of State borne by a Peer	The Cap of Maintenance borne by a Peer

H M The Queen
accompanied by
H R H The Prince Philip, Duke of Edinburgh

Pages of Honour

H R H The Prince of Wales

Woman of the Bedchamber	The Mistress of the Robes	Lady of the Bedchamber
Gold Stick in Waiting	The Lord Steward	The Master of the Horse
Lord in Waiting to Her Majesty	The Vice-Admiral of the United Kingdom	
The Captain of the Yeomen of the Guard	The Captain of the Honourable Corps of Gentlemen at Arms	
Air Aide-de-Camp to Her Majesty	First and Principal Naval Aide-de-Camp to Her Majesty	Aide-de-Camp General to Her Majesty
The Comptroller Lord Chamberlain's Office	The Gentleman Usher to the Sword of State	
Field Officer in Brigade Waiting	Silver Stick in Waiting	
The Lieutenant of the Yeomen of the Guard	The Lieutenant of the Honourable Corps of Gentlemen at Arms	

All of them are in ceremonial dress or their peers' robes. In the time-honoured tradition the Earl Marshal and the Lord Great Chamberlain walk backwards before the Queen. Inside the House of Lords, the peers and peeresses are also dressed in their parliamentary finery, including the Bishops in ecclesiastical robes and the Law Lords in robes and wigs. The Queen sits on the throne, with the Duke of Edinburgh to her left. On the right sit the Prince and Princess of Wales. Other members of the Royal Family may also be present, although the Queen Mother no longer attends as it is not the custom for the widow of a previous Sovereign to be present.

The Lord Chancellor approaches, and, bowing before the Queen, presents her with the speech which has been prepared for her. Clearly this cannot be read until the Commons, or rather the group of them chosen to represent the lower chamber in that overcrowded room, are summoned. The Queen is not allowed to enter the Commons as a reminder of the past behaviour of Charles I who violated their privileges, so the Commons have to come to the House of Lords. This requires an elaborate ritual made longer by the fact that the Commons make great play of taking their time to come. This is to make it quite clear that they know where real power lies, and are in no way over-awed by either Sovereign or peers. To summon the Commons the Lord Great Chamberlain despatches Black Rod to the House of Commons; symbolically the door is slammed in his face by a Serjeant-at-Arms as he approaches. Black Rod then knocks three times and when his identity as the Queen's messenger has been confirmed he is admitted and addresses the Speaker of the House of Commons, with the traditional formula, 'Mr Speaker, the Queen commands this Honourable House to attend Her Majesty immediately in the House of Peers.' The Speaker then leads the Commons to the House of Lords. When they are present the speech can at last be read, concluding with the words, 'I pray that the blessing of Almighty God may rest upon your counsels'.

The Queen then returns in procession to the Robing Room to remove the Crown and Robe of State. The drive back to Buckingham Palace is as majestic as the procession to the Houses of Parliament and on the Queen's arrival the mounted escort rank past and the Guard of Honour march past, giving those who have stayed outside the Palace a little extra ceremonial to compensate for their wait.

Date **Late October/early November – no fixed date. Occasionally after a General Election. See the Press for details.**

Time **11.00 a.m.**

Route **Her Majesty the Queen leaves Buckingham Palace at 10.35 a.m., travelling in the Irish State Coach accompanied by a Sovereign's Escort of Household Cavalry. The Procession route is via the Mall, Horse Guards Arch, Whitehall, Parliament Street, to the Royal Entrance beneath the Victoria Tower at the Palace of Westminster. Her Majesty arrives at 10.50 a.m.**

Order of procession **1st and 2nd Divisions of Sovereign's Escort of Household Cavalry; Irish State Coach conveying Her Majesty and the Duke of Edinburgh; the Royal Standard; 3rd Division of Sovereign's Escort; four State landaus conveying members of the Queen's Household; 4th Division of Sovereign's Escort.**

The Sovereign's Escort is made up of The Life Guards and The Blues and Royals in full ceremonial dress.

The royal carriage carrying the Crown leaves St James's Palace at approximately 10.15 a.m. It is accompanied by a Household Cavalry Regalia Escort and proceeds to the House of Lords by way of Clarence Gate and then by the processional route. Bands of the Guards' Division are posted at points along the route and play the National Anthem as the Procession passes.

Where to stand **You can stand anywhere along the processional route, but need to arrive before 9 a.m. if you wish for a key position near the Houses of Parliament.**

The other best vantage points are along the Mall and on Horse Guards Parade where you will be allowed to stand behind barriers. It is usually possible to get a good position along Whitehall even as late as 10.15-10.30 a.m. The Queen sits in the right hand side of the carriage, going and coming back, so she will be on your side for one of the journeys.

The Procession returns at approximately twelve noon. There is a rank and march past by the Sovereign's Escort, followed by the Guard of Honour, after the Queen's return to the Palace.

Members of the public are not allowed entry into the Houses of Parliament on this occasion.

The same procedure is followed on the State occasions when the Sovereign prorogues (closes) Parliament in person.

The Queen's Soldiers

THE HOUSEHOLD DIVISION

Undoubtedly the best known of all British soldiers are the men of the Household Division – the five Regiments of Foot Guards in their scarlet uniforms and bearskin caps and the Household Cavalry in their brightly polished armour and plumed helmets. These are the men who perform most of the ceremonial duties of the British Army and do it so well that many people think this is their sole function. Queen Victoria recognized their brilliance at the more theatrical side of army life when she sent them to perform at the Royal Opera House in Covent Garden. She found that the extras engaged to play the soldiers' parts lacked the correct military bearing and discipline. However, while ceremonial duties are an important part of their work they are also fully trained fighting troops who take their full share in the less pleasant aspects of army life. The mounted squadrons of the Household Cavalry (each regiment keeps 128 mounted soldiers for ceremonial duties) are only part of the story. Most of the time The Life Guards are an armoured regiment using vehicles like Chieftain tanks rather than horses and The Blues and Royals are operating armoured reconnaissance vehicles. The Foot Guards are mechanized infantry, ready to be air-lifted to serve at a moment's notice anywhere in the world.

The sense of comradeship which their proud history gives them has been a major factor in their success on the battlefield. Because of their great stoicism in the static battles of the First World War, George V honoured all privates in the regiments with the rank of Guardsman. The men of the Household Division are rightly proud of their reputation and the many battle honours they have won over the centuries, since they first fought on the Continent in 1672. Their victories are recorded on the Colours, one of which is trooped each year at the Queen's Birthday Parade.

The most recently formed regiment of Foot Guards is the Welsh Guards. They were formed by George V in February 1915. This was during the First World War when the inevitable expansion of the army offered the opportunity to have every one of the countries of the United Kingdom represented by a regiment of Foot Guards. By the end of 1915 they were fighting their first battle at Loos and have since distinguished themselves in both World Wars. Not surprisingly the regiment is famous for the quality of its battalion choir and its Rugby! Welsh Guards are recognizable by the white-green-white plume on the left of the bearskin, the buttons on the tunic being in groups of five as a reminder that it was the fifth regiment to be formed, and the leek emblem on the epaulettes and collar.

Next youngest of the Guards Regiments is the Irish Guards. These were formed in 1900 by the express order of Queen Victoria to commemorate the outstanding bravery of Irish soldiers during the Boer War in South Africa. The Irish Guards are known as the 'Micks' and although they are a comparatively new regiment they have a reputation for reckless bravery that comes not only from the fact that they were involved in nearly every major battle of the two World Wars, but also from the conduct of the many outstandingly courageous Irish soldiers who fought for Britain for hundreds of years before the regiment was formed. They always have an Irish wolfhound as a mascot to lead them on parade. Being the fourth

The Grenadier Guard being
mounted at St James's
Palace, 1840

regiment their buttons are in groupings of four; they have a shamrock on the collar and a blue plume on the right of the bearskin. The other three regiments of Foot Guards and the Household Cavalry trace their origins back to the seventeenth century, when the countries of Europe began to maintain professional standing armies rather than relying on troops raised when the occasion demanded it. It was during the reign of Charles II, restored to the throne after the death of Oliver Cromwell, that the regiments were formed much as they are today. Since then they have always enjoyed a very special relationship with the Royal Family.

The Grenadier Guards are distinguished by a white plume on the left hand side of the bearskin. On their tunic collars they have the emblem of a 'grenade fired proper' and their badge is a royal cypher surrounded by a garter. The buttons on their tunics are evenly spaced. They claim descent from the King's Regiment of Guards, a personal bodyguard raised by Charles II in 1656 while he was still in exile in Bruges. When Charles returned to England he naturally enough disbanded the old Parliamentarian army with its doubtful loyalties. In its place he raised a similar regiment of Foot Guards which was merged with the original regiment when it returned home in 1664. This regiment became known as the First Regiment of Foot Guards. It was after their defeat of the Grenadiers of Napoleon's army at the battle of Waterloo in 1815 that they acquired the title 'The First or Grenadier Regiment of Foot Guards'. Probably the most famous soldier ever to serve with the First Guards (Grenadiers) was the Duke of Marlborough, in whose French wars the Household Division served with great distinction.

The Second Regiment of Guards is the Coldstream Guards. They were initially raised under Oliver Cromwell in 1650 as part of his New Model Army. Their commander was General Monck, a brilliant soldier who had had a chequered career prior to and during the Civil War, when he had changed sides more than once. In 1660, known as Monck's Regiment of Foot, they were stationed in Coldstream on the Scottish border. Two years after the death of Cromwell when chaos had set in Monck marched them to London where he was instrumental in getting Parliament to agree to the return of Charles II. The loyal and efficient Foot Regiment which had backed up General Monck was already unofficially known as the Coldstreamers. While Charles II was disbanding the New Model Army the Coldstreamers put down a rebellion against him in the City of London. As a result an exception was made for them and on 4 February 1661 when they were ordered to lay down their arms as part of the Republican army, they were immediately commanded to take them up again as the Second Regiment of Foot Guards. They were always known as the Coldstream Guards however. Their motto, *Nulli Secundus* – Second to None – is a reminder that although the Grenadier Guards may have been the first regiment created by Charles II, they were already a regiment in 1650 and, never having been disbanded, in their own eyes they are the senior regiment of Foot Guards. They are distinguished by a red plume on the bearskin, buttons grouped in pairs and a regimental badge which is the star of the Order of the Garter.

A member of the Coldstream Guards from *A Representation of the Cloathing of His Majesty's Forces,* 1742

The Scots Guards were originally formed in 1642 by Charles I as a personal bodyguard. They served in Ireland until 1649, when they returned to Scotland to join the Scottish army of Charles II, and after Charles was forced into exile abroad after his defeat at the battle of Worcester in 1651 the regiment was disbanded by Cromwell. When Charles II was restored in 1660 they became part of the Scottish Army, known as the Scottish Regiment of Foot Guards. Queen Anne, the last of the Stuarts, had a special liking for the Scots Guards and because of their original 1642 formation tried for a while to have them listed first rather than third of the Foot Guards, but found the opposition of the outraged Grenadiers and Coldstreamers too much to overcome. After various minor changes of name they were given the simple title of Scots Guards by Queen Victoria in 1877. The uniform of the Scots Guards is distinguished from that of the other Foot Guards by the groupings of the tunic buttons into three groups of three; their collar badge is the Scots thistle, and they have no plume in their bearskin.

There are two cavalry regiments in the Household Division. The first of these is The Life Guards which is the senior regiment of the British Army. They were first formed during the exile of Charles II by eighty of his fellow exiles, under the command of Lord Gerard of Brandon. A quarter of them were always on duty to perform the two functions which are still the major concern of the mounted squadrons of that regiment today – to guard the King's residence and provide him with an escort.

When Charles returned home he had added another 600 to the Life Guard of Horse, as they were known. The present regiment results from an amalgamation in 1922 of the first and second regiments of Life Guards, themselves the result of a merger between the Horse Guards and the Horse Grenadier Guards in the eighteenth century. The uniform in which they are best known to the public and tourists is the full dress uniform worn by a mounted squadron on ceremonial occasions when guarding or escorting the Sovereign. The Life Guards have scarlet tunics and white plumes made of strips of whalebone on their helmets. The Household Cavalry are the only troops still to wear armour, albeit on ceremonial occasions, though it has not been used in battle since the end of the seventeenth century. One modern development has been the use of chromium plate rather than steel for the breast-plate, which significantly reduces the number of hours required to create the shine necessary for a perfect turn-out. The full dress uniform worn by The Blues and Royals is very similar to that of The Life Guards but the tunic is blue and the plumes in the helmet are red.

The Blues and Royals are an amalgamation of the Royal Horse Guards (the Blues) and the Royal Dragoons. The Royal Horse Guards were formed by Charles II from Cromwell's Regiment of Horse and their title The Blues comes from the colour of the livery of the Earl of Oxford whom Charles II made their first commander. Although they often shared with The Life Guards the honour of escorting and guarding the Sovereign, The Blues were not accorded the full status of Household Cavalry until 1820, when it was done as a compliment to their Colonel, the Duke of Wellington, the victor of Waterloo. The Royal Dragoons with whom they amalgamated also had a distinguished history for they were the oldest Cavalry Regiment of the Line. They had been raised by Charles II to defend Tangier which came to him as part of the dowry when he married the Portuguese Princess Catherine of Braganza, and for a while were known as the Tangier Horse. Among their many notable campaigns they took part in the Charge of the Heavy Brigade in the Crimea.

Together these seven regiments make up the Household Division, which has a unique relationship with the Sovereign. The Queen is Colonel-in-Chief of all the regiments of the Household Division.

REGIMENTAL CEREMONIES

Regiments as old as those of the Household Division naturally have traditions and ceremonies which date back for many hundred of years. Many of these involve the Sovereign or other members of the Royal Family because of their close involvement with the Household Division.

One such regimental ceremony which is common to all regiments is the

Presentation of New Colours. The Colours which are carried on special occasions are still subject to quite a lot of wear and tear, even though they are not carried into battle any longer. As a result every ten years or so the Colours have to be replaced. This is done at a special ceremony because the Colours represent the honour of the regiment and by treating them with respect members of the regiment past and present who have fought and perhaps died for their country are given the honour they deserve.

The Presentation of New Colours is usually performed by the Sovereign or another member of the Royal Family who has close connections with the regiment involved. The whole procedure follows a careful ritual. First the Old Colours are 'marched off parade'. Then the New Colours are 'marched on to parade'. The New Colours are taken out of their protective covering and draped over a drum which is laid side downwards on the ground. The Chaplain of the battalion whose Colours are being replaced then consecrates the New Colours.

When this has been done they are formally presented to the Sovereign. The Sovereign in turn presents them to the officer representing the battalion who kneels to receive them, flanked by two other officers. After the presentation the New Colours are then ceremonially 'marched past' in slow and quick time to the music of the Regimental Band.

The Presentation of New Colours takes place only rarely and occurs wherever the regiment happens to be stationed at the time. The ceremony is not open to the general public.

The Guards have two other regimental ceremonies which, while they too are not seen by the general public, emphasize the close relationship between the Royal Family and the Household Division. These are the Presentation of Leeks to members of the Welsh Guards, which takes place on St David's day, 1 March (or the Sunday nearest to it), and the Presentation of Shamrocks to the Irish Guards on St Patrick's Day, 17 March. The presentation is made by a member of the Royal Family. Princess Anne made her first solo public engagement when she presented leeks to the Welsh Guards in 1969. Queen Elizabeth the Queen Mother has for many years presented the shamrocks to the Irish Guards.

As well as demonstrating their interest in the Guards by attending their regimental ceremonies members of the Royal Family also act as colonels of the regiments. For example, Prince Charles, as Prince of Wales, is Colonel of the Welsh Guards. The Duke of Edinburgh is Colonel of the Grenadier Guards. This custom of having a colonel who is strictly honorary, while the acting head of the regiment is the Lieutenant-Colonel Commanding, is peculiar to the Guards Regiments. It dates from 1642 when Charles I authorized the 1st Marquess of Argyle to raise a Scots regiment (later the Scots Guards) which was then sent to Ireland under the command not of the Marquess but of a cousin of his whom he had appointed.

Queen Elizabeth the
Queen Mother presents a
shamrock to the Irish
wolfhound mascot of the
Irish Guards on St
Patrick's Day, 1972

THE ROYAL TOURNAMENT

Soldiers of the Household Division and other regiments, including the
King's Troop, Royal Horse Artillery, are among members of the armed
forces who take part in the Royal Tournament each year. This spectacular
display is put on at Earls Court Exhibition Centre, Warwick Road,
London SW5. A guest of honour, often a member of the Royal Family, is
present at each performance. The Royal Tournament usually takes place
in the last two and a half weeks of July (see pp. 171 and 176).

THE EDINBURGH MILITARY TATTOO

This is a display of military ceremonial and music with a distinctly
Scottish flavour, although some non-Scottish regiments, such as the
Grenadier Guards, take part. The display takes place at Edinburgh
Castle in the evening, and the later performances are floodlit. Although this
is not a royal occasion it offers a wonderful chance to see the ceremonial of

the Scottish regiments and the pageantry of Edinburgh Castle. The Edinburgh Tattoo is put on at the time of the Edinburgh Festival in August and September.

Bookings are accepted from 1 January each year, but tickets are not sent out until the beginning of March (see p. 176).

THE YEOMEN OF THE GUARD

As well as the Household Division, which has a particular responsibility for protecting the Sovereign, there are three Royal Bodyguards. The most ancient of these is the Yeomen of the Guard, which is the oldest military corps still in existence in the world. It was founded by the first of the Tudor monarchs, Henry VII, immediately after his defeat of Richard III at the battle of Bosworth in 1485. He may have taken the idea from Edward III's Yeomen of the Crown. The yeomen were a special class, not quite noblemen but with a recognized dignity and status 'Yeomen or Gentlemen just below the rank of Esquire' (in other words not eligible for knight-

hood), which made them eligible for such personal service to their king. Many of these solid, middle class men with their roots in the land had accompanied Henry during his exile in Europe and he knew he could rely on them. At a time in history when beheading was a popular way of dealing with your enemies, when political assassination was a commonplace and kings rarely felt secure even in their own beds, it is not surprising that Henry felt it necessary to provide himself with such a body of men the moment he knew the crown was his. Nowadays we associate the Yeomen of the Guard in their anachronistic Tudor uniform with ceremonial occasions but not with real battle. Because of this the Yeomen of the Guard are drawn from the ranks of distinguished retired officers, warrant officers, and non-commissioned officers of the Army, Royal Marines, or Air Force. The ceremonial role was always intended to be an integral part of the duties of the Yeomen of the Guard for Henry specified that among their other functions they were responsible for 'The upholding of the dignity and the grandeur of the English crown in perpetuity, his successors, the Kings and Queens of England for all time'.

The Queen's Soldiers

Yeomen of the Guard on duty at George v's Silver Jubilee Thanksgiving Service in St Paul's Cathedral, May 1953. The King and Queen are accompanied by some of their family (including the future Elizabeth II)

Nearly 500 years ago however the services expected of the Yeomen of the Guard were usually much more fundamental. The monarch's daily brushes with potential danger can be deduced from the additional titles carried by some of the men to this day. For example YBH after a name means Yeoman Bedhanger. During the elaborate ceremonial which always accompanied a monarch's going to bed it was the duty of this particular Yeoman to search the folds of the bed hangings for intruders. At the same time the Yeoman Bed-Goer (YBG) was checking the mattress for signs of treachery. Members of the Bodyguard would then remain on duty guarding the bed chamber through the night, a duty now performed by a more prosaic figure from the regular police force. At State Banquets Yeomen of the Guard stand at entrances to the Banqueting Hall and behind the Queen's chair – a reminder of those early days when not only did they have to act as food tasters checking for poison, but often had to oversee the cooking as well so that no foul play was done. One of the best known men to be Captain of the Guard was Sir Walter Raleigh, who was appointed by Elizabeth I. During his time in that office he took care to please the Queen by ensuring that all the members of the Guard were as handsome as she could wish. The diarist John Aubrey recounts how he nearly turned down the request from one father to make his eighteen-year-old son a member of the Guard on the grounds he was too young. However 'The Son enters, about 18 or 19, but such a goodly young Fellow as Sir Walter had not seen the like: He was the tallest of the Guard. Sir Walter Raleigh sweares him immediately; and ordered him to carry up the first Dish at Dinner, where the Queen beheld him with admiration, as if a beautiful young Giant had stalked in with the service.'

In the days when they really were an active bodyguard the Yeomen of the Guard accompanied the monarch into battle, just as they had accompanied the future Henry VII at Bosworth. During the attack of the Spanish Armada in 1588, the Yeomen of the Guard escorted Queen Elizabeth to Tilbury where she made her rousing speech ending with the words, 'I may have the body of a weak and feeble woman but I have the heart and stomach of a King, and a King of England too'. After 1743, when they guarded George II during the last occasion a monarch actually went into battle, their duties became increasingly ceremonial rather than practical. For a century the country had enjoyed internal peace and palace coups of a bloodthirsty and sudden nature were no longer a serious possibility in anyone's mind.

The occasions on which the Yeomen of the Guard can be seen are: State Banquets; searching the cellars of the Houses of Parliament two hours before the State Opening; in the Royal Gallery for the Queen's Procession from the Robing Room to the House of Lords during the State Opening of Parliament; forming the Guard of Honour at Buckingham

Palace for State visits; at the Installation of Knights of the Garter and Knights of the Bath; at the Investiture of the Prince of Wales and Investitures at Buckingham Palace; the Epiphany service at the Chapel Royal; the Royal Maundy Service; Garden Parties at Buckingham Palace; the Lying-in-State and Funeral of the Sovereign; and of course the Coronation. The eighty or so men who have the honour of belonging to the Bodyguard are therefore kept extremely busy despite the merely ceremonial nature of their duties.

The uniform worn by the Yeomen of the Guard is highly distinctive and still based on the original style of dress worn when the Royal Bodyguard was founded. It comprises a red doublet embroidered on the front in gold with the Tudor crown, Scots thistle, and Irish shamrock, below which are the York and Lancaster roses entwined and the motto *Dieu et Mon Droit.* Around the neck is a white Tudor ruff. The hat is of black velvet with a red, white, and blue band. On his legs a Yeoman of the Guard wears red breeches, red stockings, and black shoes with large red white and blue rosettes. Around his waist is a gold-embroidered cross belt with a large buckle which originally was used to help support the heavy firearm each one carried; a clear indication that these once were real fighting troops.

It is the lack of this cross belt with its very practical origin which distinguishes a Yeoman Warder (Beefeater) of the Tower of London from a Yeoman of the Guard (see p. 64).

THE HONOURABLE CORPS OF GENTLEMEN AT ARMS

The title of this Royal Bodyguard was given to them in 1834 by William IV. However, the Gentlemen at Arms have a history stretching back to 1509, when Henry VIII, following the example of his father who created the Yeomen of the Guard as a personal guard, established the 'Band of Gentlemen Pensioners'. Henry VIII, like Charles II over a century later, was anxious to emulate and, if possible, outshine, the King of France. So the title Gentlemen Pensioners was based on the title of a similar French Corps, *Les Gentilshommes de l'Hôtel du Roy ou Pensionairs* in contrast to the solidly English name of the Yeomen of the Guard. When Henry VIII formed his bodyguard they were all mounted, and sometimes called 'King's spears' as this was the weapon they carried while on horseback. Hall writes in his Chronicles for 1509:

This yere the King ordered fiftie Gentle-menne to bee Speres, every of theim to have an archer, a demilaunce, a custrell, and every spere to have three greate Horses, to bee attendaunt on his persone, of whiche bande the Erle of Exssex was Capitain and Sir Jhon Pechie Lieutenant, who endured but a while, the apparell and charges were so great, for there were none of theim, but they and their Horses were appareled and trapped in clothe of golde, silver and golde smithes woorke and their servauntes richely appareled also.

So richly dressed were they that they were probably taken by Henry VIII to the meeting with the French King at the Field of the Cloth of Gold, so that they might outshine the French. Certainly both the Earl of Essex and Sir John Pechie are known to have been present.

In about 1538 the Corps was reorganized so that there were foot soldiers as well as mounted men. The foot soldiers were issued with poleaxes. A contemporary account describes the band:

It is thought it weir convenient of the King's pleasure weyre suche that His Grace shudd appointe a gentill men waiting upon his grace with oon Capteyn . . . the gentillmen myght beire Pollaxes and goo before the King on a good order and fasshoon when soever the King goyeth to masse, evenson, or other tymes appointed.

There was always intended to be a ceremonial aspect to their duties and because of their skill on horseback the Gentlemen Pensioners represented their Sovereign at the medieval style 'tilts' or jousts, which were still an entertainment at the court. Tilting was a very popular sport with Queen Elizabeth I who liked to encourage her people in the chivalric traditions which laid such stress on loyalty and devotion to womankind in general and to the Queen in particular. Her Gentlemen at Arms were noted for their stature, good looks, and noble birth. To be Captain of such a bodyguard was a privilege to be sought after, for not only were they an outstanding body of men but their Captain could be sure of the Queen's ear.

The Pensioners saw action many times as the Sovereign's personal bodyguard. They rallied round Mary I during Wyatt's rebellion in 1554, coming into her Presence Chamber with their poleaxes in readiness, 'wherewith the ladies were very fearful, some crying and wringing their hands saying, "Alas we shall all be destroyed. What a sight to see the Queen's chamber full of armed men."' They protected Charles I at the battle of Edgehill and one of them helped to rescue the Prince of Wales (later Charles II) and the Duke of York (later James II). Sir John Hinton who was in charge of the Princes when they were attacked describes the incident '. . . being armed cap-a-pie I could do no execution on him with my sword; at which instant one Mr Mathews, a Gentleman Pensioner, rides in and with a Poleaxe decides the bussiness.'

For hundreds of years belonging to the Gentlemen Pensioners was a privilege which people were prepared to buy. Nowadays they, like the Military Knights of Windsor, are made up of distinguished retired officers. This was decided by Queen Victoria who heartily disliked the abuses which inevitably crept into a system where office was up for sale, particularly after the period under the four Georges when trading in all army posts was widespread and connived at by members of the Royal Family who themselves profited greatly. It was in Victoria's reign that the Gentlemen at Arms, as they were known by then, were last faced with the possibility of defending their Sovereign in earnest. This was during the riots of 1848, a period of civil unrest throughout Europe, when several monarchs had been forced to vacate their thrones. For a short while it was thought that rioters would attack St James's Palace where the corps has its headquarters, and the men were prepared for action, although in the event it turned out to be a false alarm. The uniform of the Honourable Corps of Gentlemen at Arms also dates from the reign of Queen Victoria, being based on the mid-nineteenth-century ceremonial uniform of another famous body of mounted soldiers, the Dragoon Guards. It consists of a scarlet coat with gold epaulettes and belt, blue trousers, and a brass helmet like that of the Household Cavalry with a central plume of white feathers. This helmet is worn all the time, even for ceremonies like the Coronation which take place in church and for which other officers have to remove their headgear. As well as the sword which goes with this style of uniform the Gentlemen at Arms may also carry the lethal looking battle-axes with which they were issued in the sixteenth century.

Two Gentlemen at Arms in front of St James's Palace, *c.* 1835

Unlike the Household Division the duties of the Gentlemen at Arms (like those of the Yeomen of the Guard and the Royal Company of Archers, the Sovereign's Scottish Bodyguard) are now purely ceremonial. There are about thirty of them and they provide an escort for the Queen at nearly every State occasion from the very grandest – the Coronation and the State Opening of Parliament – to the receptions for State Visits and Buckingham Palace Garden Parties. Along with the Household Division and the Yeomen of the Guard they have the privilege of keeping watch while the monarch's body lies in state prior to the funeral. It is unlikely they will ever again be expected to perform anything other than ceremonial functions but doubtless with their distinguished military records they would be more than equal to the challenge.

THE ROYAL COMPANY OF ARCHERS

The Royal Company of Archers is the bodyguard which escorts the Sovereign on State occasions in Scotland. This Company was formed in 1676 under the Captaincy of the Marquis of Athol and in 1704 became the Royal Company of Archers when it received a Royal Charter from Queen Anne. The formation of such a company reflected the obsession of the Scots with improving their standards of bowmanship to equal the legendary skills of the English bowmen. Although bows and arrows were no longer the major weapon by the seventeenth century, and England and Scotland were united under one king, the old obsession still rankled.

In previous centuries the necessity of encouraging men to keep up their standard of bowmanship in readiness to combat the ever-present threat of a raid from south of the border had led to many decrees from the Scottish kings. For example in 1425 James I banned the playing of football on pain of a fine of fifty shillings, on the grounds that it distracted men from their more tedious archery practice. Later kings followed his example by repeating the ban on football and also on golf, another major distraction. James I is said to have formed a personal bodyguard of archers which some claim is the true origin of the Royal Company of Archers.

On the positive side good bowmanship was encouraged by the institution of many local competitions. To this day the Royal Company of Archers shoots in many competitions each year and also plays a friendly match once every three years with the woodmen of the ancient Forest of Arden in Warwickshire. The oldest prize for which they shoot is the Musselburgh Arrow, one of the survivors of the local competitions which were once so numerous. Originally it was an open competition but is now confined to the members of the Royal Company of Archers. The prize is a silver arrow presented by the magistrates of Musselburgh and the once valuable privilege of 'grazing a goose upon the Musselburgh Common throughout the year'. Although the Musselburgh competition was begun in 1603 the prize which carries the greatest honour is the Queen's Prize. This was instituted in 1787 with a grant of £20 per year, and is shot for in the gardens of the Palace of Holyroodhouse, usually in June. The shoot is open only to guests of members of the Royal Company. Whenever possible the Queen presents this prize in person, usually when she is in residence at Holyroodhouse. The winner receives a sum of money which was originally voted by Parliament in 1870. With this money he is allowed to buy a piece of silver of his own choice – if it costs more he makes up the difference himself. This is the only prize which remains the personal property of the winner.

The Royal Company of Archers, like the Yeomen of the Guard and the Gentlemen at Arms, is made up mainly of distinguished retired servicemen. However, it is a much larger body than either of the others and numbers

A review of the Royal
Company of Archers

nearly 500. Unlike the others it has a very restrained uniform: dark green tunic with black facings, dark green trousers with a crimson stripe and a Balmoral bonnet with an eagle's feather. Officers have two feathers in their bonnets and the Captain-General three. The Secretary is distinguished by a Himalayan condor's feather which is over two feet long in his bonnet. This was brought back from India and presented to the Company by the 11th Earl of Dalhousie who was Governor General of India in the middle of the nineteenth century. Only the Captain-General wears a more elaborate court dress when he attends the Garden Party at Holyroodhouse. However, the uniform was not always so sober. On one famous recruiting march which the Company made through Leith in 1714 they wore coats of Stuart tartan lined with white, and blue bonnets with green and white ribbons.

Only a Scot may belong to the Royal Company of Archers and many of the most famous Scotsmen have been members, some, like Robert Burns, in an honorary capacity, and others, like Sir Walter Scott with his great love of historical tradition, as full members. When George IV made his State Visit to Scotland in 1822, he was the first king to visit Scotland since James II at the end of the seventeenth century. The Royal Company of Archers decided to offer their services as a personal bodyguard to him as a symbolic gesture to mark the fact that the 'Jacobites', who had for so long supported the Stuart cause, were finally reconciled with their Hanoverian kings. George IV was pleased to appoint them the privilege of being the King's Bodyguard and they accompanied him throughout the tour. When Queen Anne presented the Company with a Royal Charter she had made a condition that the Company should, if required, present the Sovereign with a 'reddendo', a Scottish feudal due which indicated their acceptance of the overlordship of the Crown. The reddendo was to be a pair (an archer's pair is three) of silver-barbed arrows. In 1822 the Royal Company presented their reddendo to George IV. Elizabeth II has been presented with a reddendo three times. Although the Royal Company of Archers has the privilege of being the 'Nearest Guard' in Scotland, they have no official capacity in England where that service is performed by the Gentlemen at Arms. However to mark their special status ten of them were allowed to represent the Company by attending the Queen at the Coronation in 1953.

Queen Victoria, like Elizabeth II, had a great affection for Scotland and it was on her State Visit there in 1842 that the Royal Company nearly came to grief when they came unwillingly into competition with a mounted regiment of Dragoons. These had taken over the escort of the Queen's carriage when she disembarked from the royal yacht earlier than anticipated. The Royal Company, none of them in their first youth, were forced to match at breakneck pace around the hilly streets of Edinburgh in order to keep pace with the carriage and its mounted escort. A contemporary wrote:

This was a source of considerable disappointment to the Archers, as it was impossible that a set of foot-guards could do their duty efficiently round a rapidly driven carriage, and amid a troop of prancing dragoons, and the presence of a hastily assembled, and therefore inefficiently restrained, mob.

When Queen Victoria's attention was drawn to the incident she took trouble to confirm once and for all that while in Scotland the Royal Company of Archers were her Royal Bodyguard, and since then their position has never been disputed, and the Royal Company of Archers can be seen on all State occasions in Scotland.

The Changing of the Guard and Guard Mounting

The Queen has five official residences, Buckingham Palace, Windsor Castle, Holyroodhouse in Edinburgh, Sandringham, and Balmoral. It would seem obvious that these should be the places where a guard is mounted. However, this would be too simple, which is rarely the case with rituals which have evolved over hundreds of years. Sandringham and Balmoral, being private residences, do not have a ceremonial guard, nor does Holyroodhouse. Buckingham Palace and Windsor, as might be expected, have a guard. But so too do the Tower of London (which has not been used since the middle of the seventeenth century as a royal residence), St James's Palace (which has rarely been the Sovereign's home although it has been the official centre of the Court since the Palace of Whitehall burned down in 1689), and Horse Guards Arch in Whitehall.

THE CHANGING OF THE GUARD AT WHITEHALL

A guard is mounted at Horse Guards because it was once the gateway to the only carriage route from Whitehall through St James's Park to the official centre of the court at St James's Palace. Although the new, wide Mall from Buckingham Palace to Admiralty Arch was opened in 1912 and is used for most State processions, the Sovereign still uses the original entrance of Horse Guards Arch on the Procession to and from the State Opening of Parliament. Only a very few people are allowed the privilege of driving through the Arch and the guarding of it is for the sake of tradition rather than security.

Since Horse Guards is the oldest entrance to the Court of St James's and the official entrance to the royal palaces, the privilege of mounting guard there belongs to the senior Royal Guard, the Queen's Life Guards which consists of the two regiments of the Household Cavalry. Very occasionally the King's Troop Royal Horse Artillery take over this privilege when The Life Guards and The Blues and Royals are training, but it is much rarer for this to happen at Whitehall than it is at the other palaces where a guard is mounted.

The ceremony of Changing the Guard usually takes place in the courtyard of Horse Guards. This is London District and Household Division Headquarters and was built in 1760 to a design by William Kent. It is on the site of the guardhouse of the old Palace of Westminster.

Occasionally during the summer months the same ceremony with the addition of a mounted band takes place on Horse Guards Parade and notices are put up in advance of this happening. The London Tourist Board Information Centre may have details of this a few days in advance (see p. 176).

The route usually followed by the Guard, who are escorted by mounted police, is from Knightsbridge Barracks on the south side of Hyde Park, across Hyde Park Corner, down Constitution Hill, along the Mall to the Horse Guards.

When the Queen is in residence the Guard is a 'Long Guard' consisting of one Officer, three Non-Commissioned Officers, and eleven troopers. A Standard is carried and they are led, both on the outward and return journey, by a trumpeter on a grey horse. Cavalry trumpeters have traditionally been mounted on grey horses so that the commander in the field could recognize them easily to give them the orders which were passed to the rest of the troopers by trumpet calls.

When the Court is not in residence at St James's, in other words when the Queen is not staying at Buckingham Palace, the Guard is a 'Short Guard' of two Non-Commissioned Officers and ten troopers. There are no officers, Standard or trumpeter.

The New Guard arrives at the Horse Guards at 11.00 a.m. (10.00 a.m. on Sundays) where the Old Guard is waiting drawn up. The Standards are saluted. Sentries from the New Guard rein back and circle round the Old and New Guard towards the guardroom.

The Corporal-of-Horse posts the two mounted sentries who look out onto Whitehall. A dismounted sentry guards the Archway and a second dismounted sentry is posted outside the guardroom. The relieved men of the Old Guard are marched back to the guardroom. The Old Guard reforms and salutes the New Guard. The Old Guard returns to barracks. The New Guard is now The Queen's Life Guard. Those who are not posted dismount and go into the guardroom.

The two mounted sentries who actually face Whitehall, and who take the brunt of interest from the tourists, are relieved every hour because of the

strain of handling a horse under those circumstances. Mounted sentries are only posted between 10.00 a.m. and 4 p.m.

Mounting the Guard, with a band, at St James's Palace, *c.* 1792

The Guard Mounting ceremony takes approximately 30 minutes, and is at 10.00 a.m. on Sundays and 11.00 on weekdays. The Queen's Life Guard leave barracks at 10.27 a.m. (or 9.27 a.m. on Sunday). At 4 p.m. The Queen's Life Guard parades dismounted.

THE CHANGING OF THE GUARD AT BUCKINGHAM PALACE AND ST JAMES'S PALACE

Because the official residence of the Court is still at St James's Palace (which includes Marlborough House and Clarence House) the St James's Palace detachment of the Queen's Guard is considered senior to the detachment which guards Buckingham Palace. The Captain of the Queen's Guard establishes his headquarters at St James's and the Colour is also lodged there. However, because Buckingham Palace has been the principal royal residence since the time of Queen Victoria, and because its vast forecourt is more suited to the ceremonial, guard mounting take place there. It is the prerogative of the Foot Guards to mount guard outside these two palaces, but in recent years they have been kept busy on operational duties particularly in Northern Ireland, and other units have taken their place from time to time. It has become something of a tradition in itself for the Gurkhas to do sentry duty at the Palace.

When the Guards are on duty spectators see the Changing of the Guard at its most colourful, for they wear their famous scarlet ceremonial dress and the bearskins which were originally introduced in the eighteenth century to give them intimidating extra height, but are now principally to impress the tourists. This uniform is extremely costly and is only kept by the guardsmen while the battalion is on ceremonial duties, being returned when the battalion returns to purely operational duties.

Each day's Guard consists of two detachments, one for Buckingham

Palace and one for St James's Palace. When the Queen is in residence, which is indicated by the Royal Standard flying above the Palace, the Guard is made up of three officers and forty other ranks. When the Queen is away the Guard is reduced to three officers and thirty-one other ranks. As they march to the Palace the Guard form three distinct groups. First comes the Regimental Band with a Corps of Drums. Next comes the St James's Palace detachment, including the Ensign, who carries the Colour which will be lodged there. Finally comes the Buckingham Palace detachment.

The Changing of the Guard
outside Buckingham Palace

11.00 a.m. The St James's Palace detachment of the Old Guard falls in at Friary Court. The Captain of the Queen's Guard inspects them. The Drummers beat 'The Point of War' as the colour is marched on. The St James's Palace detachment then marches off through Stable Yard Gate and along the Mall to Buckingham Palace.

11.07 a.m. The Buckingham Palace detachment of the Old Guard falls-in the forecourt of the Palace, where it is inspected by the Subaltern.

The Buckingham Palace detachment marches to the centre of the forecourt to await the St James's Palace detachment.

11.23 a.m. The St James's Palace detachment enters the Buckingham Palace forecourt by the South Centre Gate. The Buckingham Palace detachment present arms.

The St James's Palace detachment forms up on the right of the Buckingham Palace detachment. The drums form up on the right of the complete Guard. The Drill Sergeant checks the positioning of the guardsmen.

Meanwhile the New Guard, which includes a detachment for the Tower of London, forms up at its barracks. It is inspected by the Adjutant and handed over to the Captain of the New Guard. The New Guard marches to Buckingham Palace.

11.30 a.m. The New Guard enters the Buckingham Palace forecourt by the North Centre Gate. It halts and faces the Old Guard.

The Drill Sergeant dresses the New Guard by the right, the Band and the Corps of Drums form up behind them. The New Guard advances in slow time towards the Old Guard, while the Band plays the regimental slow march. The New Guard halts. The Old Guard present arms, followed by the New Guard.

11.33 a.m. Having paid these military compliments the Captains of each Guard bring their swords from the salute to the carry position, and advance towards each other for the ceremony of handing over the Palace keys (these are symbolic keys only).

Officers of the Buckingham Palace detachment of the Old and New Guard salute the Senior Captain on Parade. With the Non-Commissioned Officers they go to the guardroom to see to the practical side of handing over. They return and report to the Senior Captain. Meanwhile the Ensigns, with the Colours, patrol at the back.

During the ceremony the Captains of the Guards leave and enter Buckingham Palace by the Privy Purse Door to receive any special orders for the day. They then return to the main ceremony. While this is happening officers with no specific duties fall out and walk informally on the west side of the Parade.

New sentries are posted at Buckingham Palace and St James's Palace and complete orders are read to them by the Corporal. The sentries from the Old Guard at St James's Palace march into the Buckingham Palace forecourt to complete the Old Guard.

Throughout the thirty minutes which handing-over and posting sentries takes, the Band at the Centre Gate plays a selection of music. Before the Old Guard returns to barracks the Director of Music discusses with the Captain of the Old Guard the selection of music to be played as they march.

12.05 p.m. The Guards fall in and are brought to attention. The band forms up at the Centre Gate, and the Old Guard advances to the Centre Gate to the music of the regimental slow march. It right-forms to become a column of route. Military compliments are paid by the Old and New Guard to each other's Colours. Once through the Centre Gate the Old Guard marches in quick time back to barracks.

12.07 p.m. The St James's Palace detachment of the New Guard marches through the Centre Gate to Friary Court, St James's Palace where the Colour is lodged in the guardroom. The Buckingham Palace detachment marches to the guardroom.

Sentries spend two hours on duty and four hours in the guardroom. Since 1959 sentries have been posted inside the forecourt of the Palace.

The Ceremony of Guard Mounting takes place following the same procedure on most days at 11.00 a.m. However in the winter the Guard is mounted every forty-eight hours, not twenty-four. On very wet days the ceremony is considerably curtailed and is slightly less spectacular because the Guards' colourful scarlet tunics may be covered by winter coats or cloaks. The ceremony takes place in the forecourt of Buckingham Palace and can only be seen if you are up against the Palace railings. In summer as many as 5,000–10,000 tourists may be trying to see the ceremony, so it is advisable to arrive by 10.30 a.m. at the latest to get a good position.

An alternative is to see the Guards on their way from Chelsea or Wellington Barracks. They leave Chelsea Barracks at 10.55 a.m. or Wellington Barracks at 11.27 a.m.

The ceremony is carried out on a reduced scale when the Queen is not in residence, so it is wise to keep an eye on the newspapers and to go preferably when you know the Queen is in London. The Royal Standard will be flying from the Palace roof if she is in residence.

On some days in May the Foot Guards parade at Horse Guards Parade prior to changing the Guard. This parade includes a Trooping the Colour Ceremony, a reminder of the days when soldiers needed to recognize their Colour instantly in battle. Notices are usually put up at Horse Guards Parade in advance.

For details of this and of the route to be taken by the Guard from their barracks, telephone the London Tourist Board Information Centre (see p. 176).

THE CHANGING OF THE GUARD AT WINDSOR CASTLE

William the Conqueror took over the existing Saxon castle at Windsor and rebuilt it a few miles away on a hill to increase its effectiveness as a fortress. It was just one of many castles such as Dover Castle and the Tower of London, built by him and his successors to keep a firm grip on the newly conquered nation. When the castles were built they were intended not just for housing soldiers but as fortified residences for the nobles who did the king's peacekeeping for him. William decided to keep Windsor for his own use as a residence, not just because of its strategic importance but because of the good hunting to be had in the surrounding forest. Ever since Windsor has been a royal residence, favoured by some monarchs more than others, and at times even used to imprison them.

Since it was largely rebuilt by Henry II in the twelfth century the castle has undergone many structural changes particularly those made for Charles II who wanted to make it the English equivalent of Versailles, and George IV. Although it is medieval in its origins the medieval appearance that can be seen today is a Gothic pastiche which is almost entirely due to George IV's architect, Wyatville, who renovated and altered it in the early nineteenth century at a cost of more than a million pounds.

Queen Victoria and Prince Albert spent their honeymoon at Windsor and it remained a favourite residence until the Prince died at Windsor of typhoid fever in 1861.

Elizabeth II uses Windsor a great deal as a week-end retreat which is conveniently near London, and the Great Park is well suited to many of the Royal Family's favourite occupations, such as show-jumping, polo, and carriage racing. Twice a year the Court moves officially to Windsor and the State Apartments are brought into use. Windsor Castle gave its name to the present Royal Family, when in 1917 George V decided that the surname Saxe-Coburg was not suitable for a monarch whose country was at war with Germany. Since then the Royal Family have been the House of Windsor.

Guard Mounting takes place at Windsor Castle at 11.00 a.m. with a Guard from the Battalion of Foot Guards stationed at Elizabeth Barracks, Pirbright. (They still march up from Victoria Barracks, Windsor, their usual home, which is being rebuilt over a period of years.)

When the Court is in residence the Guard mounts in the Quadrangle. The Guard then consists of one Officer, six Non-Commissioned Officers, one Drummer, and twenty-one Guardsmen.

Otherwise the ceremony takes place outside the guardroom by the Henry VIII Gate in the winter months and on Castle Hill in the summer. On these occasions the Guard is made up of one Officer, four Non-Commissioned Officers, one Drummer, and fifteen Guardsmen. Sentries are posted at the Advanced Gate, St George's Gate, the George IV Gate, the Brunswick Tower, the Quadrangle, and outside the Guardroom.

There is usually a military band or a Corp of Drummers to make the ceremony more colourful.

THE CHANGING OF THE GUARD AT THE TOWER OF LONDON

Like Windsor Castle the Tower of London was originally built as a fortress by William the Conqueror on the site of an existing fortification. Up until the last war it was used for military purposes, including the incarceration

Morning Parade at the
Tower of London in 1880,
with the band of the
Grenadier Guards

of Rudolf Hess and the execution by firing squad of Corporal Josef Jakobs, a German spy. The Tower was frequently used for executions, and many royal kings and queens, princes and princesses have lost their heads there, including two of Henry VIII's wives, Catherine Howard and Anne Boleyn. Edward V and his brother were murdered there at the instigation, it is said, of their uncle, Richard III, who is also popularly believed to have had his brother, the Duke of Clarence, drowned there in a butt of Malmsey wine. The Tower is full of mementoes of its bloody past, including the axes used by the executioners and a brass plate on Tower Green which marks the place where the scaffold stood.

No monarch has lived at the Tower since James I at the beginning of the seventeenth century, although his grandson, Charles II, observed the old tradition of spending the eve of his coronation there. Nowadays the Tower is known principally as a tourist attraction, but the Guard is still mounted not only because it remains in theory a Royal Palace, but because the priceless Crown Jewels are housed there in the Waterloo Barracks.

The Guard, which is provided by the same regiment which finds the Queen's Guards for Buckingham Palace that day, is mounted on Tower Green at 11.30 a.m. – daily in summer and every other day in winter. It consists of one Officer, five Non-Commissioned Officers, and fifteen Guardsmen. The ceremony is based on the larger scale ceremony which takes place in the forecourt at Buckingham Palace.

During the day a sentry is posted at the guardroom and at the entrance of Queen's House. In the evening additional sentries are posted to protect the Jewel House and its approaches.

The Ceremony of the Keys at the Tower of London

At 10 o'clock every evening the tradition of locking up the Tower takes place. This is called the Ceremony of the Keys because of the unvarying ritual which surrounds it, and it is one of the oldest ceremonies in the world since something similar has been performed for over 700 years. At approximately 9.50 p.m. the Chief Yeoman Warder wearing a scarlet coat, black velvet Tudor bonnet on his head, and carrying a lantern and the Queen's Keys for the Tower, emerges from the Byward Tower. He joins an Escort of the Guards Regiment which is on duty at the Tower that day, made up of a Sergeant of the Guard and three Guardsmen. One Guardsman carries the lantern for the Chief Yeoman Warder as the group then proceeds on its rounds. Whenever they pass a sentry he presents arms as a sign of respect for the Queen's Keys.

One by one the Chief Warder locks the outer West Gate and each of the vast medieval wooden gates at the Middle Tower and the Byward Tower. As they reach the Bloody Tower Archway on their way back, the sentry challenges them and an exchange takes place, which has probably not altered for the last 700 years.

The Chief Yeoman Warder and an Escort of Guards doing the rounds of the Tower of London during the daily Ceremony of the Keys. Photographed in 1898

The sentry challenges by calling, 'Halt! Who comes there?'
The Chief Warder replies, 'The Keys.'
'Whose Keys?' calls out the sentry.
'Queen Elizabeth's Keys.'
To which the sentry replies, 'Pass Queen Elizabeth's Keys, all's well.'

The Chief Yeoman Warder and his Escort then continue up the slope through the gate of the Bloody Tower. On the Broad Walk steps the Guard is drawn up under the command of the Officer, and with the Drummer standing behind them. As the Chief Warder and the Escort draw to a halt the officer gives the order 'Guard and Escort, present Arms'. After this has been done, the Chief Warder takes two steps forward, removes his Tudor bonnet and cries, 'God Preserve Queen Elizabeth', to which everyone else replies, 'Amen'. The Last Post is then sounded, and the ceremony comes to an end as the clock strikes ten.

After the ceremony the Chief Warder takes the Keys to the Governor of the Tower who lives in Queen's House. This was built by Henry VIII in the early sixteenth century and was the last lodging of Anne Boleyn before her execution on Tower Green.

After midnight no one can enter the Tower of London without knowing the password which is changed every day.

A similar ceremony for unlocking the gates each morning was discontinued just before the First World War.

THE YEOMEN WARDERS

The Yeomen Warders are descended from those in medieval days charged with securing the Tower's gates. As the Tower began to be ousted as a royal residence by the more comfortable palaces, further to the West of London, the Sovereign no longer required a personal bodyguard there. However, the Tower still needed protecting so in 1509 Henry VIII left a detachment of the Yeomen of the Guard (formed in 1485 by Henry VII) there to carry out guard, and other, duties under the Constable and they became known as the Yeomen Warders. (They now have the affectionate nickname Beefeaters from the French word *buffetier* – someone who waits at the table.)

Their dress and status must, however, have declined, for we find the Duke of Somerset securing for them from Edward VI in 1550 their position as Extraordinary Members of the Yeomen of the Guard. This honoured a promise he made to them when he was imprisoned in the Tower, as a reward for their kind treatment of him. It is from this time that the scarlet and gold State dress worn by both Bodies derives. The only difference between the two is that the Yeomen of the Guard still wear a cross belt over the left shoulder, which is a reminder of the time when they needed it to support their heavy and cumbersome firearms when escorting the Sovereign.

The Yeomen of both Bodies are armed with swords and carry eight foot long 'partisans' (halberd pikes) which date from the time of the formation of the Yeomen of the Guard by Henry VII in 1485. The Chief Warder carries a Mace topped by a silver replica of the White Tower. They appear in full State dress carrying these weapons on State occasions, when a new Constable of the Tower is installed, for Beating the Bounds, a tradition at the Tower which takes place on Ascension Day every third year and at Easter, Whitsun, and the Sunday before Christmas when they provide the Escort for the Governor to 11 o'clock Matins. (The public may attend all services in the Chapel Royal.)

On other days the Yeomen Warders wear an Undress Uniform of blue with red piping authorized by Queen Victoria. It is less spectacular but more suited to the practical duties they have to perform every day. For the Yeomen Warders' main duty is still to guard the Tower. They also organize the visitors to the Tower, serving it as faithfully now that its primary function is a tourist attraction as they once served it when it was a royal residence and a traitor's prison. The Yeomen Warders, like the Yeomen of the Guard, the Gentlemen at Arms, and the Company of Archers, are retired military men, in this case Warrant Officers and Senior Non-Commissioned Officers. Like the other bodies they have several uniquely named officers including, not surprisingly, the Yeoman Gaoler, who is second in command and carries the ceremonial axe. One whose function is still more than symbolic today is the Yeoman Raven Master. It is his job to feed the ravens who are sent in as young birds, usually abandoned fledglings, and are kept with their wings clipped at the Tower to keep them away from the urban area. There is also an old legend that says the White Tower and the Empire will fall if the ravens ever leave the Tower. So in a small way the Yeomen Warders still protect the monarch's interests as they did in the turbulent days after the Wars of the Roses when Tudor monarchs set them up as a 'private guard of faithful fellowes'.

The Ceremony of the Keys is not a public ceremony. However, tickets for a total of 70 people are available each evening on application to the Governor of the Tower of London. There is a long waiting list and applications should be made at least two months in advance. (Not more than 7 people per family group.) Applications should be made in writing, enclosing a stamped self-addressed envelope (see p. 176).

The Queen visits the Tower from time to time to attend a service at the Chapel Royal of St Peter and Vincula. On these occasions she is escorted by the Governor of the Tower and there is an escort of Yeomen Warders in State dress. Visits are announced in advance in the Court Circular pages of the Press.

Trooping the Colour

Trooping the Colour attracts a crowd of thousands and a television audience of millions every year. The spectacle of soldiers of the Household Division marching with perfect precision in slow and quick time to the music of massed regimental bands never fails to impress even the most cynical observers. For foreign visitors it exemplifies all that is best and most moving about British pageantry and proves, if it needed proving, that the monarchy is an essential feature of the tourist industry.

Each move in the intricate display of marching and counter-marching, all of it based on previous battle manoeuvres, is carefully rehearsed for weeks beforehand, and the rehearsals monitored on video-tape. If it were not for the almost obligatory incident of a Guardsman fainting under the strain of standing perfectly still the Foot Guards in their scarlet uniforms and bearskins, the cavalry in their glittering breastplates and plumed helmets, and the mounted musicians in their seventeenth-century gold coats, would seem just like mechanical soldiers. Russell Braddon in his history of the Household Division relates one officer's advice about fainting, 'There are all sorts of anti-fainting devices. Wriggle your toes, flex your knees, avoid tight bearskins, and think what the RSM'll do to you if you do faint.' More practically barley sugar is issued to the men once they have donned their ceremonial uniform. Much of the 'choreography' of the marching and counter-marching of the bands which lasts for almost an hour is too complicated to record on paper, but is handed down by word of mouth, in particular the elaborate 'spin-wheel' manoeuvres. The soldiers who take part in the ceremony are men whose work is not only ceremonial. Like the men who guard Buckingham Palace they are ordinary serving soldiers. many of them recent recruits, who may well have returned only recently from service abroad. Altogether nearly 1,500 men and over 200 horses are involved in the Parade and their achievement of excellence richly deserves the praise which is always heaped on the event.

Trooping the Colour is now almost always associated with one particular event; the birthday of the Sovereign, who is the Colonel in Chief of all seven regiments of the Household Division. For this most spectacular 'Trooping' the Colour of a battalion of one of the regiments of Foot Guards is paraded in celebration. The regiments take their turn for this honour in strict rotation. However, Trooping the Colour does take place in a less spectacular fashion on many other occasions, such as the presentation of new Colours to a regiment. These parades are not open to the public although it is usually possible for families of the men involved to see them take place.

66

The reason why scaled down versions of the Sovereign's Birthday Parade go on throughout the year lies in the origin of the ceremony which was once of extreme practical importance. In the past, the flag bearing the identifying Colour of the company or battalion was the symbol to which the men rallied during the heat of the battle, or when they needed to assemble quickly to offer a united front against attack. In the late seventeenth and eighteenth centuries the smaller more personalized companies were being reorganized into larger units, with men recruited on a permanent basis. This was happening all over Europe with the result that armies like the French army, reorganized under Louis x i v, had greatly increased their efficiency. In England Charles ii on his Restoration in 1660 created the country's first standing army from his own personal bodyguard and disbanded units of Cromwell's Model Army.

Soldiers who had been used to fighting in small units now had to become familiar with new *Regimental* Colours. A visual sign was especially important at this time because so many of the men fighting with the British armies abroad were foreign mercenaries who might misunderstand verbal instructions. In order that the entire regiment should recognize its own Colours and respond immediately it was vital that everyone was totally familiar with them. So it became customary to troop the Colours through the ranks every evening and particularly before a battle, before setting them up at battalion headquarters for the night.

The term 'trooping' the Colour comes from the tune or 'troop' which was played as the Colour was paraded. The music made the ceremony more impressive and helped create the right state of mind for battle. It explains why military music is such an important feature of the modern ceremony. It is not an extra to give the spectators a more enjoyable time, but an integral part of the procedure.

Until 1751 each regiment had three Colours. There are now two – the Sovereign's Colour and the Regimental Colour. It is the Queen's Colour which is trooped at the Sovereign's birthday parade. The Colours of the five regiments of Foot Guards are the reverse of those of the Infantry regiments. The Foot Guards have a Sovereign's Colour which is basically crimson, with a royal crown and regimental device in the centre. The Foot Guards' Regimental Colour is a Union Jack. An infantry regiment has a Union Jack as the Sovereign's Colour. Inscribed on both Colours are the names of famous battles in which the regiment has distinguished itself. For the regiments of the Household Division the Colours, which are presented to them personally by the Sovereign, are a symbol of their unique relationship. Thus Trooping the Colour is a particularly fitting birthday tribute to their Colonel in Chief.

Colours were last carried into battle during the Crimean War, 1854–56. The ill-fated Charge of the Light Brigade, at the battle of Balaclava, is usually romantically portrayed as the men were galloping down the valley with Lord Cardigan at the head holding the Colour aloft. Nowadays the Colours serve no directly practical purpose but they symbolize the traditions and heroism of the regiment and its pride in its achievements.

Trooping the Colour is only part of the Sovereign's Birthday Parade. The ceremony is also a royal review by the monarch of the troops. Charles II for example used to review his newly founded Foot and Horse Guards on Putney Heath. A personal review by the monarch was a good reminder of the personal allegiance due from each individual soldier at a time when unswerving loyalty could not be taken for granted. However the development of Trooping the Colour into a purely ceremonial occasion really began a hundred years prior to the Crimean War in 1755. In that year the parade was performed in honour of George II. George had many failings, including an irascible character, but he was not short of personal courage. He was popular with the army for like all Hanoverians he loved every aspect of military life, particularly the uniforms, and he liked nothing better than a good war! As mentioned earlier, he was the last British monarch to lead his troops into battle. This was at the British victory over the French in 1743 at the battle of Dettingen. (Although George did slightly mar his triumph by wearing a Hanoverian and not a British uniform.)

In 1805, the year of Nelson's great victory at Trafalgar, Trooping the

George V at the Trooping the Colour ceremony in 1934

Colour was instituted as an annual event to celebrate the birthday of George II's grandson, George III. Except during the period of George III's mental instability from 1811 to 1820, when Britain had a Prince Regent, and during the First and Second World Wars, the ceremony has been an annual event ever since.

While Queen Victoria was on the throne she was generally holidaying at Balmoral on her actual birthday, 24 May. It therefore became customary to hold the parade on a separate 'official' birthday, which used to be a Thursday. The concept of an 'official' birthday has persisted but is now either the first or second Saturday in June, to avoid the busy weekday traffic. Queen Victoria preferred to leave the Birthday Parades to her male relations and gave up appearing at them altogether after Prince Albert's death. She did from time to time review her troops on horseback, a fact which upset some of her advisers who considered it unseemly. A carriage would have been more dignified and, before she married Albert, would have made it possible for a chaperone to accompany her on this mainly male occasion. A popular verse on the subject went:

> I will have a horse, I'm determined on that,
> If there is to be a review,
> No horse, no review, my Lord Melbourne, that's flat,
> In spite of Mama and of you.

George II was the last British monarch to lead his troops in battle – at the Battle of Dettingen in 1743. Painting by John Wootton

Although she was loath to appear publicly with her Household Division, Victoria was as interested in them as her predecessors. Our present Queen has inherited the Hanoverian love of military minutiae. It is well known by her Guards that she takes a keen interest in their performance at the Parade. Indeed after any ceremonial occasion it is usual for the Queen to send 'notes' to whoever is responsible for the arrangements, be it the Prime Minister or a Major General, on small details which were not up to standard. All of which is hardly surprising since no one has as much unbroken experience of these procedures as the main participant herself.

The Trooping the Colour is the only occasion on which the Queen appears publicly on horseback, and when she rides side-saddle. For this she wears a specially adapted skirt. With the skirt is worn the tunic of the Regiment of Guards whose Colour is being trooped and a tricorn hat with the plume of the same regiment. A male monarch wears the uniform of Colonel in Chief of the appropriate regiment. In 1981 the Queen ably demonstrated her superb horsemanship even under the handicap of riding side-saddle when she swiftly brought her horse under control after a young man in the crowd had fired a gun at her containing blanks.

Trooping the Colour has a special significance for Elizabeth II for it was her appearance in her father's place at the 1949 Trooping that alerted the world to George VI's rapidly deteriorating health, and initiated for Elizabeth an escalating number of public engagements in his place prior to his premature death in 1952.

Trooping the Colour is a spectacular and breathtaking display of military precision. Here is a detailed scenario of the ceremony itself.

Ticket holders should be in their places at Horse Guards Parade at 10.30 a.m. when eight Guards of the Foot Guards, each consisting of three Officers and seventy Non-Commissioned Officers and Guardsmen, are formed up across the parade ground. (Eight is the usual number of Guards of the Foot but for various reasons it might be reduced – to a minimum of five. This would, of course, affect the pattern of the ceremony.) Numbers 1 to 5 Guards are on the west side of the parade ground, facing the famous Horse Guards Archway. Number 1 Guard forms the Escort for the Colour. Numbers 6 to 8 Guards are on the north side of the parade ground with their backs to the old Admiralty Buildings. The massed bands of the Guards Division, together with the Corps of Drums of the battalions on parade, are formed up in front of the garden wall of 10 Downing Street.

The Queen's Colour which is to be trooped is posted in front of Number 7 Guard. When the line has formed the officers fall in.

If Her Majesty Queen Elizabeth the Queen Mother is to watch the ceremony she now drives onto Horse Guards Parade and is received with a royal salute, while the National Anthem is played. Her Majesty then drives to Horse Guards Building to watch the parade with other members of the Royal Family, from the window above the centre arch.

Her Majesty the Queen, attended by the Royal Procession and escorted by the Sovereign's Escort of the Household Cavalry, leaves Buckingham Palace at 10.40 a.m. and processes down the Mall, arriving at the parade ground at precisely 11 a.m. As the clock strikes, the National Anthem is played and the Royal Horse Artillery in Hyde Park fires a salute of 41 guns, which can be heard on the parade ground.

The Queen inspects the Guards and the Sovereign's Escort, while the massed bands play a slow then a quick march. As she passes the Colour the Queen salutes.

The Queen then returns to the front of Horse Guards Building and remains unmoving on her horse for the next hour and twenty minutes. The Field Officer gives the command, 'Troop'. Three drum beats and a roll of drums give the signal to the massed bands and drums for a musical display of counter-marching in slow and quick time, beginning with the traditional slow march 'Les Huguenots'. It is this demonstration of skill and discipline which has made Trooping the Colour a world famous spectacle. Regiments not taking part in the parade are represented in the bands. During the Quick Troop one side drummer leaves the massed bands and marches to the right of the line.

When the bands stop playing the lone drummer beats 'Drummer's Call', while the command of the Escort for the Colour is taken from the Captain by the Lieutenant. The Escort marches to the centre of the parade ground and halts facing the Colour. They march to the traditional tune 'The British Grenadiers'. This tune is used by all regiments at this stage of the parade because the right flank of every battalion used to be a Grenadier company. The Regimental Sergeant Major, who only carries a drawn sword on this one occasion, hands over the Colour to the Ensign who is recognized by his white colour belt. For the rest of the ceremony the Ensign will carry the heavy Colour. The escort presents arms to receive the Colour and the four Non-Commissioned Officers at the flanks turn out-wards and port arms to symbolize the Escort's protection of the Colour'

The Colour is now trooped down the line of Guards. The massed bands at this stage perform a complicated spin and wheel using the technique that is handed down by word of mouth. The Escort returns to its original position and the Captain resumes command.

The Guards form up and march past the Queen at the saluting base in slow and quick time. The Colour is brought to the front of the Escort and is lowered in salute as it passes the Queen. The Guards then reform in their original positions. Now it is the turn of the Household Cavalry. The Sovereign's Escort walks and trots past the saluting base and returns to

position. The Royal Salute is given. The Household Cavalry leave Horse Guards Parade and each Guard forms in two divisions ready for the march back to Buckingham Palace. The leading division consists of the men who will form the Queen's Guard for the day.

The Field Officer rides over to Her Majesty and informs her that her Guards are ready to march off. Her Majesty places herself at the head of her Guards, and leads them back along the Mall to Buckingham Palace.

At Buckingham Palace the two detachments of the New Queen's Guard form up opposite the Old Queen's Guard. The remainder of the Guards march past the Queen who takes a final salute in the centre gateway. The King's Troop, Royal Horse Artillery, and the Sovereign's Escort then rank past Her Majesty, led by the massed mounted bands.

The Queen turns and rides between the Old and New Queen's Guards into the Palace. The daily ceremony of the Changing of the Guard then proceeds as usual, to music by the massed bands.

Every year there is a fly past by the Royal Air Force at 1 p.m. (unless it is prevented by the weather) when the Queen may appear on the Buckingham Palace balcony.

Date **1st or 2nd Saturday in June (see Press)**
Time **11.00 a.m.**
Place **The ceremony takes place at Horse Guards Parade, between Whitehall and St James's Park.**
Route **Procession begins at Buckingham Palace. Proceeds down the Mall to Horse Guards Parade. The procession returns along the same route.**
Tickets for the Birthday Parade **There are approximately 7,000 places at Horse Guards Parade for members of the public who wish to watch the Sovereign's Birthday Parade. However an average 100,000 people apply for seats each year, so applications are put into a ballot. Applications for tickets should be made between 1 January and 28 February (see p. 176). There is a charge for tickets which are limited to two per applicant. Within a few weeks you will be sent an official ballot form which you must complete and return.**

The ballot is held in mid-March and if you hear nothing further by 31 March then you have been unsuccessful and should try again the following year. If you are successful then you will be notified by post. The cost per seat is £5-£50 (1982) which you must pay after you have been notified.
Second Rehearsal **On the Saturday prior to the Trooping of the Colour there is a full rehearsal at which some members of the Royal Family will be present. If you are not successful in the ballot you can be considered for the rehearsal if you wish, and there is space on your ballot form to indicate this. Tickets for the second rehearsal cost £3.00 (1982) and again you will be notified before 31 March if you have been successful.**
First Rehearsal **This rehearsal is held two weeks before the ceremony. Again a ballot has to be held. Naturally this is the easiest to get tickets for. Usually no members of the Royal Family will be present, but if you are successful the tickets are free.**

Elizabeth II outside Buckingham Palace taking the final salute after Trooping the Colour in 1952 (the first following her Accession)

If you do not have tickets but want to see the procession, it begins leaving Buckingham Palace at approximately 10.15 a.m. The Queen and her Escort can be seen leaving Buckingham Palace and proceeding along the Mall at 10.40 a.m. Anywhere along the Mall will give you a magnificent view of the bands and regiments, members of the Royal Family travelling in open landaus, and the Queen as she rides side-saddle along the centre of the processional route, followed closely by the Prince of Wales and the Duke of Edinburgh. Although some people arrive as early as 5 a.m. to be sure of a front position you should still get a reasonable place at 9 a.m. It is advisable to arrive before 10 a.m. when the police start to close the Mall.

The procession returns at approximately 12.20 p.m. Those with a place outside Buckingham Palace will see the Queen's final salute and the Guard Mounting as well as the procession.

The Queen usually appears on the balcony of Buckingham Palace at 1 p.m. for the fly past by the R.A.F. which follows a line along the Mall and directly over Buckingham Palace.

Beating Retreat

Although there are never enough tickets to satisfy the demand to see the Queen's Birthday Parade, there are other less well known opportunities to see the exceptional military precision and musical skills of the Guards. On several evenings every year, at the end of May or the beginning of June, they Beat Retreat at Horse Guards Parade. This ceremony is sometimes performed by regiments other than the Guards (occasionally the Royal Marines perform it in honour of the birthday of their Captain General, the Duke of Edinburgh) but it is the Guards who seem to have the extra magic which people want to witness.

Beating Retreat is a display of marching and counter-marching on a grand scale second only to the Queen's Birthday Parade. Like the Birthday Parade it involves mounted musicians, massed bands, trumpeters, and pipes and drums. It is the retreat of daylight and the onset of night which is 'beaten' or signalled as the regiments are called back to camp at nightfall. The ceremony ends with the Evening Hymn and the sounding of the 'Last Post' as darkness falls.

Beating Retreat usually takes place in the presence of a member of the Royal Family and the proceeds are donated to charity.

Date **Annually, usually the first Tuesday, Wednesday, and Thursday in June, but may be the last Tuesday, Wednesday, and Thursday in May.**

Opposite, top: Queen Elizabeth on her way to the State Opening of Parliament

Opposite, bottom: The cross belt and cuirass of an officer of The Blues and Royals (left); and (right) the cross belt of a Drum Major of the Irish Guards

Overleaf: Trooping the Colour. Queen Elizabeth the Queen Mother arriving by carriage for the ceremony (top); and the Colour of the Grenadier Guards being lowered in salute as it passes the Queen (bottom)

Times **See Press. Usually after 6.30 p.m. Floodlit after 9.30 p.m.**
Place **Horse Guards Parade.**
Tickets **Attendance at Beating Retreat is by ticket only. Tickets may be bought in advance, preferably in January or February, although tickets may be available up to the time of the performance. Seats cost £3.50 or £3.00 or you can stand for 50p (1982). The ticket office is in the street opposite Big Ben and you can call in for tickets or write with your remittance, stating how many tickets you want and enclosing a stamped self-addressed envelope (see p. 176).**

Royal Gun Salutes

These salutes, which are also customary in countries other than Britain, are a form of military compliment. As mentioned earlier the logic of what at first seems a rather aggressive form of greeting is that by firing the guns you prove they are empty and cannot be used to attack. This gesture has become ritualized and seldom varies.

Royal Salutes at Hyde Park are fired by the King's Troop, Royal Horse Artillery, who were given their title by George VI. They are part of the regular army, stationed in London, but for the purpose of the Royal Salutes, and also for their impressive display in the musical drive at the Royal Tournament, they wear a nineteenth-century uniform which makes them look like heroes from a romantic novel. It consists of blue pantaloons with a red stripe, a blue jacket frogged in yellow with a red collar, spurred black boots, white gloves, and a busby with red bag, white plume, and yellow lines.

Salutes are fired at twelve o'clock at Hyde Park unless they are timed to coincide with a specific event such as the arrival of a State Visit. Shortly beforehand the six 13-pounder guns, each drawn by six horses with three riders and a mounted escort, are brought at high speed onto the exercise ground. The guns, which were first used in action in 1904 and last used in action in 1942, are skilfully assembled at lightning speed just as if it was in the heat of battle. A Royal Salute of 21 guns, plus an extra 20 because Hyde Park is a Royal Park, is then fired, the rounds coming at ten-second intervals from each gun in turn.

Royal Salutes at the Tower of London are fired by the Honourable Artillery Company. They usually fire a 62 gun salute, which is calculated as follows: 21 for a Royal Salute, 20 because the Tower is a royal palace, and 21 rounds as a loyal tribute from the City of London and in recognition of

Previous page: A view of the Henry VII Chapel in Westminster Abbey showing the banners and stalls of the Knights Grand Cross of the Order of the Bath

Opposite: A page from the Garter Book of William Bruges, the first Garter King of Arms, showing him with St George (c. 1430); and (inset) part of the Garter Procession at Windsor Castle.

The Honourable Artillery
Company firing a Gun
Salute from the Tower of
London

its unique status. These salutes are usually timed for 1 p.m. This is because
the HAC is not part of the regular army but a volunteer unit which is part
of the Territorial and Army Volunteer Reserve. Since most of them have
regular jobs it is easier for them to be available at the lunch hour of 1 p.m.
rather than at 12 p.m.!

The HAC is the oldest volunteer unit still in existence in the army. It
received its charter from Henry VIII in 1537. Famous City men who have
served with the HAC include Sir Christopher Wren, Samuel Pepys, and
John Milton. Since 1660, when Charles II formally forgave them for
supporting the Roundheads during the Civil War, they have had as their
Captain General either the Sovereign or the Prince of Wales. In 1685 they
changed their title from the Fraternity of St George to their present name.

Because, in theory, the City of London still preserves a certain amount
of autonomy the HAC takes over as the Sovereign's Bodyguard in the
City and provides the Guard of Honour when the Sovereign visits the
Tower of London. The HAC also provides the bodyguard for the Lord
Mayor of London during his procession and at State banquets and similar
important functions. This bodyguard is taken from a section specifically
formed for ceremonial duties called 'The Company of Pikemen and
Musketeers'. This was formed very recently, in 1955, but their seventeenth-
century uniform, complete with helmet and breastplate, is a reminder of
the HAC's long history.

The HAC has been responsible for Royal Salutes at the Tower of
London since 1924 when the regular army unit responsible, the 'Battery-
within-the-Tower', was disbanded.

Place Royal Salutes are fired in London in two places, in **Hyde Park**, almost opposite the Dorchester Hotel, and at **Tower Wharf**, by the Traitors' Gate at the Tower of London. Occasionally a salute is fired at **Woolwich** or at **Horse Guards Parade**.

Dates The Royal Salutes are always fired on: Accession Day, 6 February; the Queen's Birthday, 21 April; Coronation Day, 2 June; the Queen's Official Birthday, 1st Saturday in June; the Duke of Edinburgh's Birthday, 10 June; the Queen Mother's Birthday, 4 August; as the Queen arrives at the House of Lords to open Parliament in November. In addition Salutes are fired at the moment the Sovereign is crowned, if the Queen prorogues Parliament in person, for a State visit, and on Remembrance Sunday.

The Salute for the State Opening of Parliament is fired only in Hyde Park. The Remembrance Sunday Salute is fired by the King's Troop on Horse Guards Parade. Otherwise the Royal Salutes are fired at both Hyde Park and the Tower of London.

Times On most occasions the King's Troop fire in Hyde Park at twelve noon and the Honourable Artillery Company fire at the Tower at 1.00 p.m.

For the Queen's Birthday Parade they fire at 11.00 a.m., the exact moment when Her Majesty arrives at Horse Guards Parade.

On Remembrance Sunday a gun fired by the King's Troop from Horse Guards Parade at 11.00 a.m. indicates the beginning of the Two Minutes' Silence. A second is fired at 11.02 a.m. to mark the end.

For a State visit the Royal Salute is fired at the moment the distinguished visitor steps off the train at Victoria Station. Times are announced beforehand in the Press. Usually 12.30 p.m.

For the State Opening of Parliament the Royal Salute is timed for the arrival of the Queen at the House of Lords at 11.00 a.m.

As well as the regular dates and times additional salutes may be fired to mark a special occasion, such as a royal birth or wedding. These salutes are announced beforehand in the Press or in the published programme.

What to see It is always an interesting event to watch, and members of the public are able to watch free of charge in Hyde Park. At Hyde Park and the Tower you can stand within a few yards of the guns.

The Hyde Park salute is particularly spectacular. Six 13-pounder guns, each drawn by six horses with three riders, are driven to the Park, and up to 70 horses and riders take part in the salute.

The number of rounds fired for a Royal Salute is 41 in Hyde Park and 62 at the Tower of London.

The Sovereign's Parade, Sandhurst

This is the annual passing out parade of the Royal Military Academy at Sandhurst which usually takes place during the last week in July. The entire college assembles to watch the Senior Officer Cadets parade for the last time before receiving their Sovereign's Commissions. This is done in the presence of either the Sovereign or a senior member of the Royal Family.

The Colour is trooped and the Soverign takes the salute as the cadets march past. There is then a short address by the Sovereign after which the outstanding cadet of the intake is presented with the coveted 'Sword of Honour'. A second award, the 'Monarch's Medal', is awarded to another cadet; however, the two awards are not a first and second prize as the criteria by which the candidates are selected are quite different.

The ceremony ends as the military bands play 'Auld Lang Syne'. After this the Senior Division marches from the parade ground up the steps of the Grand Entrance of the College. Traditionally the Adjutant then follows them up the steps on horseback and into the College itself. This feat is a virtuoso display of horsemanship.

Tickets are available only for the families of cadets taking part.

The Epiphany Service

One of the most attractive of the annual royal ceremonies is the Epiphany Service at the Chapel Royal at St James's Palace. This takes place on 6 January, the day when Christian churches all over the world celebrate the Feast of the Epiphany. The word epiphany comes from the Greek word meaning manifestation; the Feast is a celebration of the manifestation of Christ to the Gentiles, in the form of the three kings who came from the East following a star which led them to Bethlehem. The gifts they brought, gold, frankincense, and myrrh, were gifts appropriate to a royal person and symbolized their acceptance of the fact that Christ was a greater king than any of them. Not surprisingly the Epiphany became a feast day with special significance for the monarch.

It has always been customary for the Sovereign to make gifts to the church or the poor on several important dates in the church calendar, such as Maundy Thursday, and on important state occasions like the Coronation. These gifts vary but those which are offered on the Feast of the Epiphany are, naturally, gold, frankincense, and myrrh. This tradition evolved soon after Britain was converted to Christianity and for hundreds of years it was customary for the monarch to present the gifts in person whenever possible. Eventually the ceremony became associated with the Chapel Royal at St James's Palace when it became a principal royal palace in the middle of the sixteenth century. However, although the service continues to take place there each year, in the middle of the eighteenth century the Hanoverian kings, who were never over-enamoured of English customs, allowed the personal presence of the monarch to lapse. In this century several traditional ceremonies, such as the Garter Service, have been revived with the monarch taking part. In 1932 George V restarted the tradition of the Sovereign's being present at the Maundy Service, which has similar origins to the Epiphany Service. Despite this the Epiphany Service remains a royal ceremony which takes place without the Sovereign, who is represented by two of her Gentlemen Ushers. This may now be because during the New Year period the Royal Family leave London to stay at Sandringham in Norfolk. The fact that the monarch always used to be present is indicated by the presence of the Royal Body-guard, the Yeomen of the Guard who stand on either side of the aisle dressed in their scarlet and gold Tudor uniform.

The richness of the occasion is enhanced by the costume worn by the church's famous choir. 'The Gentlemen and Children of the Chapel Royal'. The adults of the choir wear red cassocks with white surplices and white bow ties. The children wear scarlet tunics decorated with gold braid which are strongly reminiscent of the uniform of the Yeomen of the Guard. With the tunic they wear red knee breeches, black stockings, and black buckled shoes.

The Epiphany Service

The Children of the Chapel Royal (St James's Palace) after Early Service, 1936. Their black armbands show them to be in mourning for George V

Because the Maundy Service is also a Chapel Royal service, although it is now held in Westminster Abbey or a major provincial church, the same choir attends the Sovereign wherever it may be held. Accompanying the Sovereign has always been a duty of the Chapel Royal Choir. They went with Henry v to France and sang before the battle of Agincourt in 1415, and journeyed as part of the retinue of Henry viii when he met the French king François i at the Field of the Cloth of Gold in 1520. The choir has sung at many royal marriages, including that of Queen Victoria and Prince Albert, and that of their son – the future Edward vii.

Today as in previous centuries the gifts offered by the Queen at the Epiphany Service are the traditional ones of gold, frankincense, and myrrh. One of the Gentlemen Ushers chosen to represent the Queen carries the gold, in the form of twenty-five gold sovereigns, on a silver gilt salver like the one used to carry the Maundy money. On a similar salver the second Gentleman Usher carries the frankincense and myrrh. Then escorted by three Yeomen of the Guard, and preceded by the Serjeant of the Vestry carrying a silver gilt wand of office, the Gentlemen Ushers take the offerings to the altar where they bow three times (three being one of the symbolic numbers in Christianity) and place the gifts on an alms dish carried by the sub-dean.

The offerings are dedicated by the Dean of the Chapels Royal (there is also a Chapel Royal at Hampton Court and one at the Tower of London) who is always, *ex officio*, the Bishop of London. The whole ceremony takes place within the framework of an Anglican Holy Communion service.

After the service the twenty-five sovereigns are returned to the Bank of England who supplied the gold. The cash they give in return is given towards charities connected with the Chapel Royal. The frankincense is given by the Chapel Royal to an Anglican church which uses incense and the myrrh is given to Nashdom Abbey, where it is also used to make incense.

Place **St James's Palace, the Chapel Royal.**
Date **6 January (Feast of the Epiphany).**
Time **11.15 or 11.30 a.m.**
The Epiphany Service, like most other services at the Chapel Royal, is open to the public. Since the church is very small and some of the seats are reserved, it is necessary to arrive early to be sure of a place.

The Royal Maundy

Every year on Maundy Thursday (the day of penance before Good Friday) the Queen distributes alms known as the Royal Maundy.

The ceremony from which the present day Royal Maundy derives is not unique to Britain. It is a widespread Christian tradition rooted in the episode during the Last Supper when Jesus washed the feet of his disciples. Similar acts of humility have been performed ever since by those seeking to act according to his words 'A new commandment I give unto you, that ye love one another as I have loved you', and it is usually accepted that the actual word Maundy comes from the Latin word *mandatum* – a command. A ritual equivalent to our own Royal Maundy has long been one of the customs of the Eastern church and only a few years ago Pope John XXIII chose to demonstrate his own humility in a similar ceremony.

In England the symbolic washing of the feet of poor people, usually accompanied by gifts of money, food, or clothing was a gesture made not only by the Sovereign. Many others kept up the practice including Henry VIII's divorced wife, Catherine of Aragon, who was allowed to keep her own Maundy on condition she did so in a private capacity and not as the King's wife. Cardinal Wolsey, himself at one time Henry VIII's Lord High Almoner, until he fell out of the King's favour, liked to keep his own Maundy.

During the Middle Ages kings did not usually perform the ceremony themselves but instructed high ranking clerics to do so on their behalf. However, in the thirteenth century Edward I, Edward II, and Edward III made it their practice to participate in the Maundy personally. By the sixteenth century the Tudor monarchs, eager to highlight their customary magnificence by this annual act of humility, to impress with the generosity of their gifts, and to emphasize their continuity with the traditions of past monarchs, turned the ceremony into a more or less annual event. Thus the Maundy ceremony became the Royal Maundy which is kept in a similar fashion by Elizabeth II today.

Because Maundy ceremonies are clearly based on the events of the Last Supper they usually include the donation of alms to twelve deserving people who correspond to the twelve Apostles. Sometimes this number is made up to thirteen, the extra person representing the Angel who by tradition is supposed to have been present at the Last Supper. The Royal Maundy is different because the money distributed and the number of people who receive it are related to the monarch's age and not to the number of Apostles. As far back as 1363 Edward III, who was then fifty years old, distributed alms to fifty poor men. By the sixteenth century the number of pennies given by the Tudor kings and queens, like the number of recipients, was based on the age of the monarchs concerned plus one extra penny to represent the 'year of grace' which it was hoped God would grant them. An exception was made for the boy king Edward vi who was only ten years old at the time of his first Royal Maundy. For the first two years of his reign the number of pennies and recipients was made up to twelve to symbolize the Apostles.

Royal Maundy money from the reigns of George ii (*top*) and Elizabeth ii (*bottom*)

Our present Queen, like all sovereigns since the sixteenth century, also distributes a Maundy related to her age. As many men and as many women as the Queen has years, plus one extra for the year of grace, receive the same number of pennies. Those present at the service who count the number of recipients may notice that they do not always tally exactly with the Queen's age. This is because those who are too old or infirm to come in person may have their gifts taken to their homes.

One aspect of the Maundy ceremony which has been dropped along the way is the washing of the feet, or *pedilavium*, (from the Latin words for foot and wash). Although this still happens in some places where the Last Supper is commemorated in a similar fashion, the British monarchs discontinued the practice around the end of the seventeenth century. The Catholic monarch James ii who was deposed in 1689 was almost certainly the last to do so, at the 1685 Royal Maundy held in the Chapel Royal of the Palace at Whitehall. However, there are some very obvious reminders in the present day ritual to show that washing the feet of the poor was once an integral part of the procedure. The fragrant nosegays of violets, primroses, cheerfulness, and white stocks carried by the Queen, the Lord High Almoner, and other principal participants were originally very necessary to combat the overpowering smell which emanated from the pressing throng of unwashed humanity. It was also believed that these posies warded off the plague – a thought which was probably uppermost in the mind of Charles II as he washed the feet of his poor subjects during the plague-stricken years of the 1660s.

The linen towels still worn by the Lord High Almoner and his assistants originally had a practical purpose for it was the unenviable task of these officials to give the feet a preliminary wash in scented water before the monarch performed the ritual ablutions. For hundreds of years the towels

Children of the Royal Almonry with traditional linen towels and posies. Late nineteenth-century photograph taken at a Royal Maundy Service

A Yeoman of the Guard carrying a dish of red and white purses containing the Maundy alms. Photograph *c.* 1895

which had been used for drying were then given away as part of the alms. Later it became usual for them to be kept as souvenirs by those who had helped officials, but since 1883 the same set of towels has been retained and used at every subsequent ceremony.

It was not only the linen towels and Maundy money itself which made up the gift in past centuries. There were also much needed gifts of food and clothing. In 1556 for example, each recipient was given a length of cloth, a pair of shoes, the apron and towels used for the *pedilavium* and enough food for four people, including a bowl of wine. In 1699 the additional gifts consisted of two yards of broadcloth, four yards of linen cloth, new shoes, a salt cod, salmon, two dozen herrings, and a bowl of wine. It also came to be expected that the gown worn by the monarch during the ceremony should subsequently be presented to the most deserving person present. Mary Tudor, whose humility and religious fervour were so great that she conducted the entire *pedilavium* on her knees, seems to have had no regrets about parting with her rich, fur-lined gown afterwards. Her more practical sister, Elizabeth I, was deeply attached to every item in her splendid wardrobe and preferred to give away twenty shillings to each person in lieu of that particular gift. Nowadays this £1 'robe redemption money' forms part of the total gift.

So three purses are distributed by the Queen: a white purse with red strings containing the specially minted Maundy money; a red purse with white strings containing the 'robe redemption money' plus money in lieu of the food gift; and either a green purse with white strings (for the women) or a white purse with green strings (for the men) containing the money in lieu of clothes. The silver Maundy dish used for the first distribution and the Fish Dishes, so called because of their decoration, which are used for the second distribution, can be seen with the rest of the royal Regalia in the Jewel House at the Tower of London.

After 1698, when William III distributed his own Maundy, the Royal Maundy took place without the presence of the monarch, who was deputized for by the Lord High Almoner. In 1932 George V revived the custom becoming the first monarch for over 230 years to take part in person. By that time it had become customary to hold the service at Westminster Abbey. When Elizabeth II became Queen, the Maundy ceremony was the first public ceremony she carried out after her Accession. She initiated the idea of alternating the ceremony between the Abbey and other major churches. As a result the Royal Maundy was distributed outside London for the first time in 200 years when the Queen visited St Alban's Cathedral in 1957. By taking this moving and colourful ceremony outside London, and by almost always distributing the alms in person, the Queen has revitalized one of our most ancient royal ceremonies. The Yeomen of the Guard are always in attendance and those who are able to get a place in the cathedral or immediately outside are rewarded by a low-key but impressive display of pageantry with its origins going back nearly 2,000 years.

The Royal Maundy generally alternates between Westminster Abbey and a provincial cathedral, usually one in an area where the Queen already has a visit scheduled or one which has a special anniversary to commemorate. Details of time and place appear in local press and in the court circular printed in *The Times*. Places in the church are usually allocated at the discretion of the organizers, and availability will depend on the capacity of the church.

Both before and after the ceremony there is plenty to see outside as well. The Yeomen of the Guard line up outside the entrance and the Queen appears with others who have taken part in the service and usually takes the opportunity to stroll informally through the crowd.

THE ORDER OF THE SERVICE

The service begins with two separate processions up to the High Altar while a hymn is sung. The first procession is the cathedral procession, headed by the cathedral cross. It is in the following order:

The Children of the Chapel Royal, St James's Palace

Choristers of the cathedral
Gentlemen of the Chapel Royal, St James's Palace
Cathedral clergy and the Dean of the cathedral escorting the Queen and
the Duke of Edinburgh

The second procession represents the Royal Almonry and is in the
following order:

Clerk of the Cheque and Adjutant
Officer commanding the Queen's Bodyguard of the Yeomen of the Guard
Yeomen of the Guard carrying the alms dishes which contain the purses
Yeomen in Attendance
Children of the Royal Almonry
Officials of the Royal Almonry (including the Secretary and Assistant
Secretary who wear towels around their waists and over their right
shoulders)
The Lord High Almoner and Sub Almoner

The Service begins with the words from St John's Gospel 'A new commandment I give unto you, that ye love one another as I have loved you.'
This is followed by prayers, a psalm, more prayers, and a reading from
chapter 13 of St John's Gospel describing how Jesus washed the feet of his
disciples.

The first distribution of alms is then made. For this the Lord High
Almoner and the Sub Almoner remove their copes to reveal the symbolic
linen towels over their surplices. They conduct the Queen to the Secretary
of the Almonry, the Assistant Secretary and the Yeoman carrying the
alms dish.

The Queen then passes down through the church distributing purses
to the women who are seated on the south side. As she returns she hands
purses to the men seated on the opposite side.

A second lesson is read from the Gospel of St Matthew, chapter 25 before
the Queen makes a second distribution of purses, and the service concludes
with prayers, a hymn, a blessing, and the National Anthem.

Date **Always takes place on the Thursday before Good Friday. (31 March 1983 –
Westminster Abbey.)**
Time **Service in cathedral 11.30 a.m.–12.20 p.m. (When out of London the Queen
is usually flown to the nearest airport and is then driven to the church or cathedral,
arriving approximately 11.23 a.m. It is possible to find out the route from the local
newspaper.)**
What to see outside **Outside the Abbey or cathedral, Yeomen of the Guard in bright
scarlet tunics line up to form a Guard of Honour – in itself a memorable sight. The
Queen and the Duke of Edinburgh frequently visit a local school, or lunch with local**

dignitaries at the Civic Centre, giving people a further opportunity to see them. Full details are given in the local newspaper well in advance.

It is wise to arrive by 10.00 a.m. at the latest for a good view, although the general public are never allowed too close to the cathedral – the spaces being reserved for Yeomen, etc and on some occasions the police have appeared to outnumber the crowd!

To be present at the Royal Maundy Service in the Abbey or cathedral it is necessary to apply to the Dean of the church concerned. Buckingham Palace say that it is left entirely to the Dean's discretion who attends. Of course many seats will be reserved for church and local officials and for family and friends of the recipients of the Royal Maundy.

Founder's Day at the Royal Hospital Chelsea

The Royal Founder who has been commemorated every year since 1692 by the Founder's Day Parade is Charles II. He is remembered in this way for the generosity and goodwill that prompted him to found the hospital which, as the Latin inscription over the colonnade declares, is 'for the help and comfort of old soldiers broken by age and war'. From what we know of him Charles II probably did have a kind heart, but it is likely that practical considerations weighed as much as kindness when in December 1681 he donated £2,000 of his 'more particular private money' and issued a Royal Warrant to found a hospital 'for the relief of such Land Souldiers as are or shall be old, lame or infirme in ye service of the Crowne'.

On his Restoration to the throne in 1660 Charles had disbanded Cromwell's New Model Army and in its place created England's first real standing army based around the nucleus of his personal bodyguard. These regiments evolved into the regiments of the Household Division as we know them today. However 300 years ago there were no invalidity pensions and retirement pensions to compensate for a lifetime's work in the service of the Crown and after twenty years recruiting was dropping off as the novelty of the restored monarchy began to fade. Charles therefore founded the hospital (the word is used in its old-fashioned sense of hospice) as an inducement to potential soldiers. Like so many of Charles II's projects it was based on an idea of the French king whom he longed to emulate, Louis XIV, who had founded the Hôtel des Invalides in Paris. The building in Chelsea is itself a major London monument, though its beauty should come as no surprise since it was built by Charles's Surveyor General of Works, Sir Christopher Wren.

Charles's brother, James II, who succeeded him in 1685, continued his work by expanding Wren's building with two further wings to accommodate retired guardsmen and cavalrymen and the building was completed in 1692. It was James who approved the famous scarlet uniform and tricorn hat which distinguish the inmates of the hospital so clearly. He also introduced proper army pensions of 2p a day! These pensions were for all ex-servicemen, but then, as now, those living in the hospital surrendered their army pension in exchange for all their living expenses, clothes, food, and entertainment facilities. Only a small drink allowance was included and over the years In-Pensioners went to great lengths to increase the money available for beer, even selling their clothes and keeping chickens among Wren's gracious colonnades! Those men who surrendered their

Founder's Day at the Royal Hospital Chelsea

pensions in return for living in the hospital acquired the title of In-Pensioners and this is how they are known today. The Out-Pensioners, for whom there was no room, kept their pensions and made their own arrangements. Over the years the number of In-Pensioners has remained at around 450. Although they are all ex-servicemen they are now civilians whose only duties are to attend church and pay parades.

Founder's Day is celebrated on 29 May (or as near to that date as possible) because it was Charles II's birthday and the date of his Restoration to the throne in 1660. It is also known as Oak Apple Day as a reminder

Standing under the statue of Charles II, covered in oak leaves, Princess Anne takes the salute at the Founder's Day Parade, Royal Hospital Chelsea

Queen Mary talking to
Chelsea Pensioners on
Founder's Day, 1929

of the famous incident without which there would have been no Charles II, and, consequently, no Royal Hospital. After his defeat at the battle of Worcester in 1651 he was hidden in the Boscobel oak by the loyal Penderel family, and so eluded Cromwell's troops and escaped to France. Those who go to watch the Founder's Day ceremony are encouraged to wear small twigs of oak in their lapels as do all the staff and the In-Pensioners themselves. In the centre of the main Figure Court where the actual parade takes place is a statue by Grinling Gibbons of Charles II in the guise of a Roman Emperor and this too is garlanded with oak leaves for the occasion.

Those Pensioners who are physically active parade for inspection round three sides of the square and facing the statue of Charles II. They make a fine sight in their scarlet coats and black tricorn hats, the ceremonial dress, or number 1 uniform which is worn instead of the dark blue everyday uniform. Their fellow Pensioners who are too infirm to take part actively stay seated behind them. Music is provided by a band from one of the Guards regiments. The parade is usually taken by a member of the Royal Family or high-ranking military figure, and after the inspection the Pensioners march past to the tune 'The Boys of the Old Brigade'. As they pass the person taking the salute the Pensioners salute using the hand furthest away. This is a reminder of the period when knights lifted their visors with the hand furthest from the person they were saluting to show their intentions were honourable and they were not trying to obscure their faces.

When the March Past is over the Pensioners re-form in two columns facing the Reviewing Officer and receive a short address from him (or her). After this the Governor of the Royal Hospital calls for 'Three Cheers for our Pious Founder' and then another three cheers for the Sovereign. The Pensioners standing and sitting, enthusiastically respond and wave the black tricorn hats which on special occasions like this replace the forage caps they wear ordinarily.

The parade is then dismissed but the band continues to play as the distinguished visitor is taken to inspect the hospital. After this it is open for inspection to the rest of the public who are able to see inside the building which contains many fine paintings. Meanwhile in the panelled Great Hall the Pensioners are given a special lunch which traditionally features plum duff and a double ration of beer.

Date **29 May – Oak Apple Day** (or as near as possible).
Place **Figure Court** (by statue of King Charles II), **Royal Chelsea Hospital.**
Time **10.45 a.m.**
Because of the great demand for tickets to see this ceremony and the limited amount of space, it is now by invitation only – usually the families of the pensioners. ('It's harder to get to see this than get a ticket for the Trooping the Colour', said one member of staff.) Members of the public can, however, visit the hospital free of charge, weekdays 10.00 a.m.-12.00 p.m. and 2.00 p.m.-6.00 p.m., Sundays 2.00 p.m.-6.00 p.m. (or dusk). Sunday chapel services are Communion Services at 8.30 a.m. and 12.00 p.m. and the Morning Parade Service at 11.00 a.m. All these services are open to the public.

Founder's Day at the Royal Hospital Chelsea/ Remembrance Sunday

Remembrance Sunday

On Remembrance Sunday the nation remembers with gratitude all those soldiers in Britain, the Commonwealth, and the Empire who have given their lives for their country. In particular they remember the million and a half dead from the two World Wars. At the ceremony at the Cenotaph the Sovereign presents a wreath as a token of the gratitude of the country and Commonwealth as a whole. The memorial itself is uncompromisingly plain and unembellished. Designed by Sir Edwin Lutyens to commemorate the dead of the First World War, the words inscribed on it, 'The Glorious Dead', became an equally fitting tribute to those who died in the Second World War less than thirty years later.

Although throughout the country Remembrance Day has had less impact as the years have passed and a generation has grown up who can remember nothing of either conflict, the Remembrance Day ceremony in which the Queen takes part is still a very moving occasion for those who are there. The First World War ended officially on the eleventh hour of the eleventh day of the eleventh month and this has traditionally been the day when those who died are remembered. Since 1956 the ceremony has been held on the second Sunday in November, when the disruption to traffic in Whitehall is less important. Crowds begin to gather early in the morning in order to be in Whitehall itself. The area around the Cenotaph is reserved for detachments representing all the armed forces, the Royal Navy, the Royal Marines, the Army, the Royal Air Force, the Territorial and Army Volunteer Reserve, the Royal Auxiliary Air Force. On the north side of the Cenotaph are the detachments of ex-servicemen and women, some of whom are veterans of the First World War and some of whom have only recently done service in places like Northern Ireland. For those of the crowd who cannot get near enough to see what is going on the proceedings, including the service, are relayed over loudspeakers.

Those who have taken part in a Remembrance Sunday service have experienced a rare sense of unity and comradeship among the crowds which combines great patriotism with great sadness. These emotions are underlined by the massed bands of the different services which play appropriately sombre music throughout.

Those who arrive too late to be in Whitehall can go to the Mall to watch the procession of cars carrying members of the Royal Family, who leave Buckingham Palace at approximately 10.35 a.m. They go first to the old Home Office building in Whitehall and those members of the family who

The Queen lays a wreath at the Cenotaph on Remembrance Day, 1980

are not laying a wreath remain there to watch the proceedings from the upstairs windows of the building. At one minute to eleven the Queen and any of her family who are taking part in the ceremony leave the Home Office building and arrive at the Cenotaph at the precise moment that Big Ben begins to strike the hour. At exactly the same time men of the King's Troop, Royal Horse Artillery fire a single gun from Horse Guards Parade which can be heard along the length of Whitehall.

This signals two minutes when the whole of London seems silent except for the twittering of the pigeons – the two most moving minutes of the whole day. Then a second round is fired by the King's Troop to mark the end of the silence and the Buglers of the Royal Marines play the 'Last Post'.

As the bands play the Queen steps forward to lay the first wreath. She is followed by other members of the Royal Family, the leaders of the political parties, representatives of Commonwealth governments, all the fighting forces, the Merchant Navy and Air Services, the fishing fleets, and the Civilian Services.

Afterwards a short service is conducted by the Bishop of London, who is Dean of the Chapels Royal. The music is by the massed bands and the choir of the Chapel Royal at St James's Palace, who look rather incongruous in their bright scarlet and gold among all the funereal black.

When the service finishes the Trumpeters of the Royal Air Force sound 'Reveille'. The bands play the National Anthem and the Queen, government ministers, Commonwealth representatives, and all those who have laid wreaths then depart. Finally, the ex-servicemen and women march past the Cenotaph as the massed bands play tunes familiar to them from both World Wars.

Many of the crowd then go on to Westminster Abbey where there is a Garden of Remembrance divided into plots representing different regiments. There they plant small crosses, each one a tribute to a friend or relative who died in one of the World Wars. Like the formal ceremony at the Cenotaph the thousands of little crosses, too many to be counted, are proof that those who died have not been forgotten by their country or their friends.

Date **The second Sunday in November, on or about 11 November.**
Place **The Cenotaph in Whitehall.**
Time **11.00 a.m.**
As with so many State and royal ceremonies the best view of the proceedings is to be had by watching the television. However the Remembrance Service is infinitely more touching and emotional for those who are actually present.

Places around the Cenotaph itself are reserved for representative detachments of the armed services and the north side is allocated to ex-servicemen and women.

The rest of Whitehall is open to the public and the service is relayed over loudspeakers. To get a place in Whitehall you should arrive about 8.00 a.m. Some people

start arriving at about 6 a.m. The royal party can be seen driving down the Mall from Buckingham Palace to Whitehall at 10.35 a.m. approximately and the King's Troop, Royal Horse Artillery fire a gun at Horse Guards Parade at 11.00 a.m. and 11.02 a.m.

THE FESTIVAL OF REMEMBRANCE

The day before Remembrance Sunday a Festival of Remembrance is held at the Royal Albert Hall, South Kensington. This is nearly always attended by the Queen and other members of the Royal Family, who can be seen arriving shortly before it begins at 7.30 p.m. The Festival takes the form of a short service together with military music, much of it nostalgic, and military pageantry. At the end of the evening the 'Last Post' is sounded and words from a poem by Laurence Binyon are spoken:

> They shall grow not old as we that are left grow old,
> Age shall not weary them, nor the years condemn,
> At the going down of the sun, and in the morning,
> We will remember them.

Scarlet poppy petals, a reminder of the terrible battlefields of Northern France and Belgium, are then allowed to fall from the roof. Each one represents a life cut short. The thousands of petals drifting gently to the ground are a poignant reminder of the reality of war, despite the pageantry and strong sense of comradeship.

The Festival of Remembrance can be seen on the television but tickets for the Royal Albert Hall itself are only available to ex-members of the armed forces. These tickets are allocated through the many Royal British Legion clubs throughout the country. Because the demand for tickets is so high each club is allowed two tickets which they allocate on a rota basis.

A similar Service of Remembrance is held at the Royal Albert Hall on the afternoon of the same day. This is open to everyone. There is no member of the Royal Family present. Tickets for this, and details of both events are available from Royal British Legion Head Office (see p. 176).

Royal Visits to the City of London

The City of London, as it increased in wealth during the Middle Ages, increased in power and prestige. Initially it was very much subject to the authority of the king and William the Conqueror's fortress, the Tower of

London, was a constant reminder of that authority. But as the City and its merchants became richer the Crown's expenses, particularly for foreign wars, were escalating. As a result the Crown often needed to look to the wealth of the City for support. Richard Whittington, for instance, the real life Lord Mayor of London on whom the pantomime Dick Whittington is based, lent Henry IV and Henry V huge sums of money to carry on their wars against the French at the beginning of the fifteenth century. Loans of that size did not come for nothing and Sir Richard Whittington, despite being a commoner, was made a member of the influential Privy Council which advised the king.

The City gradually whittled away at the authority of the Crown over hundreds of years, and as London became not only the wealthiest city in the country but also the heart of a wealthy overseas empire as well, London's privileges quickly outstripped the concessions gained by other towns. The City became famous for its independence from the Crown which needed the money it made. During the Civil War the City of London was a powerful enemy to the king and only supported the Restoration of Charles II when it was made clear that his power would be severely curtailed by Parliament. In addition the City was careful to emphasize its own independence and privileges under the restored monarch. Even today the City keeps its own police force as a sign that it continues to be responsible for law and order within its own boundaries. Similarly it preferred to raise its own army units, like the Honourable Artillery Company (see p. 76), rather than risk the unwelcome entry of the Crown's soldiers within its jurisdiction. Nowadays troops wishing to enter the City of London must first obtain the permission of the Lord Mayor. Only a select number of regiments is permitted to march through the City streets in the traditional recruiting fashion 'with Drums Beating, Colours Flying and Bayonets Fixed'. When one of these privileged regiments or corps (The Blues and Royals, the Honourable Artillery Company, the Grenadier Guards, the Coldstream Guards, the Queen's Regiment, the Royal Regiment of Fusiliers, and the Royal Marines) seeks to enter in this fashion the City Marshal rides to meet them and formally give them permission saying, 'I have it on the authority of the Lord Mayor to receive and escort your battalion through the City'. Like all restrictions the lifting of it acquires the status of a great privilege. So the City was able to honour the Royal Air Force when it allowed it to march in this fashion along the route to the Battle of Britain services held in St Paul's in 1953 and 1958.

It is not surprising therefore that there should be a ceremony to mark each occasion when the Sovereign, whom the City so long regarded as an uneasy combination of feudal overlord and enemy of its freedoms, enters the City boundaries. Nowadays the ritual may seem fairly empty for both Sovereign and City are subject to a bureaucratic central government.

George v, accompanied by
Queen Mary, on his Silver
Jubilee tour in 1935
accepting the Pearl Sword
from the Lord Mayor at
the boundary of the City
of London

Yet, as with so much of the country's ceremonial, it is an outward form of a concept which is as crucial today as it was when King John was forced to sign the Magna Carta in 1215 – that government in the form of the Crown, or any other institution, has to be ready to respect the rights and freedoms of its subjects.

The boundary where the City of London starts and the City of Westminster ends is marked in several London streets by a Griffin. Although the ceremony in the past has been performed at several points on this boundary, often on the Embankment, it is now customary for it to take place at Temple Bar in the Strand (near the East end of the Law Courts at the junction with Middle Temple Lane). Nowadays the Temple Bar is marked by two statues, one of Queen Victoria and one of her son the Prince of Wales, later King Edward vii. This memorial was set up in 1880 by J. E. Boehm, a popular sculptor of the time. It replaced the arched gateway which was removed in 1878 to Theobalds Park, where it has sadly deteriorated. There has recently been a campaign to restore this fine monument and return it to London, though clearly it could not be replaced in the Strand with its high volume of traffic. The entry ceremony occurs only when the Queen visits the City on State occasions. Shortly before the Queen is due to arrive at Temple Bar the Mayoral party sets out in four cars. The first car in the procession contains the City Marshal and a Deputation of the Court of Common Council. The second car carries the two Sheriffs (this office is even more ancient than that of Lord Mayor) and the Remembrancer, the third car has a Deputation of the Court of Alder-

George VI and Queen
Elizabeth, preceded by the
Pearl Sword, coming down
the steps of St Paul's
Cathedral after a wartime
service there, 1943

men. In the fourth car are the Lord Mayor, his Sword Bearer, the Common
Cryer, and the Serjeant-at-Arms who carries the mace. On their arrival
they are met by representatives of Messrs Child and Co. at their banking
house. The entry ceremony takes place just within the City boundary to
the north of the memorial. Shortly before the Queen arrives the Lord
Mayor and his party take their places. A crimson cord is held across the
road by City of London policemen to symbolize the now absent Temple Bar.

Troops of the Queen's Escort of Household Cavalry arrive first and pass
to the south of the monument, halting just past the junction with Chancery Lane. As the Queen's Procession approaches the cord is withdrawn
and she drives just within the City limit.

As soon as the Queen's car or carriage has drawn to a halt the Lord
Mayor, who is dressed in the Crimson Velvet Reception Robe, receives the
Pearl Sword from his Sword Bearer (who is easily distinguished by his
round fur hat). The Sword Bearer carries this sword before the Lord Mayor
on the most important ceremonial occasions. It is nearly four feet long and
takes its name from its pearl-encrusted scabbard. The Pearl Sword was a
gift to the Mayor and Corporation from Elizabeth I in 1571 when she
opened the first Royal Exchange. Holding the sword the Lord Mayor
approaches the Queen and offers it to her hilt first. Although the Sovereign's
stopping at the boundary indicates a proper respect for the freedom of the
City, the Mayor's offering the sword is equally a token of his acceptance of
the ultimate authority of the Crown.

Until the time of Charles I it was customary for the monarch to retain

95

the sword throughout the visit, but succeeding monarchs have followed his precedent of simply touching the sword and indicating its immediate return to the Lord Mayor. When this has been done the Pearl Sword and the mace, which have been reversed in deference to the Sovereign, are raised again. The Royal Procession then continues, preceded by the Lord Mayor and the Aldermen. When they reach their destination the Lord Mayor himself carries the Pearl Sword in front of the Queen.

There is plenty of room for the public to watch the ceremony at Temple Bar which accompanies the Royal Entry into the City. State occasions when the Queen will enter the City are announced beforehand in the court circular in the Press.

The Heralds

During the Middle Ages it was important for fighting men, both in battle and in the jousts and tournaments with which they amused themselves when they were not fighting, to be recognizable to their friends and their enemies. The tournaments had begun as hard practice for the field of battle, but over the centuries they became great festive occasions, and the fighting more of a stylized sport than an out and out free for all.

The officials responsible for the practical running of these tournaments were called heralds. They performed the tasks which we now delegate at sporting events to marshals and umpires. Since it was in their interests to be able to identify their charges quickly and efficiently it was they who developed the system of identification which then took their name – heraldry. The system of heraldry was based on a custom common to many countries and civilizations, that of decorating the shield of a warrior. The designs which evolved in the Middle Ages from about the end of the twelfth century and which the heralds were responsible for became known not as 'shields' but as 'coats of arms' or simply 'arms', because they were also used to decorate the loose tunics (and surcoats) which knights began to wear over their chain mail.

Tournaments were arranged locally by the nobility of the area. The greatest tournaments were those organized under the aegis of the king. After Edward III founded the Order of the Garter in the middle of the fourteenth century tournaments became more popular than ever, an indispensable part of the code of chivalry because they allowed individuals to prove their prowess. All those who organized tournaments kept their own heralds. The chief of each set of heralds was known as the 'King of Heralds' and later 'King of Arms'. Today's heralds still carry titles which can be traced back centuries. They identify the areas and people for whom they once arranged the tournaments. Inevitably the heralds responsible for the king's tournaments and the coats of arms resulting from them became paramount, so that eventually all coats of arms were devised and controlled by the royal heralds. This made sense then as it does today, for the Crown is the fount of honour and the coats of arms which made that honour instantly identifiable were best devised by those whose knowledge of the system was unparalleled. On a more practical level it meant the king could keep strict control of the nobles who were always seeking greater independence.

Since most honours were hereditary the system developed in complexity to be flexible enough to accommodate the various changes resulting from births, marriages, and inheritances. By the end of the fifteenth century the pattern of heraldry was established in the form it has today. It differs from the ancient forms of shield identification from which it originated by the fact that it has to conform to a definite system and is controlled by a single authoritative body – the heralds of the College of Arms.

The type of people who required such clear personal identification, from the king down to the most recently created knight, were people of what was known as 'gentle birth'. Clearly a peasant eking out his existence on the land had no need for such refinements. As a result the coats of arms which developed as a means of identification became inevitably bound up with the prestige and honour of the person or body concerned.

By the end of the fifteenth century the numbers and titles of the heralds were much as they are today, except that there was a King of Arms for Wales. The College of Arms became an official part of the Royal Household when it was incorporated by a Royal Charter of Richard III in 1484. They were re-incorporated in 1555 by Mary I and rehoused in Derby House, Queen Victoria Street, in the City of London.

Today the College of Arms still occupies the building which replaced that original house after it was destroyed in the Great Fire of London in 1666. The officers of arms retain the titles which were confirmed by the 1555 charter. First among them, because he is associated with the oldest Order of Chivalry – the Garter, is Garter King of Arms. This name dates back to 1415 when it was created by Henry V who appointed William Bruges as the first holder of the title. As well as being the most important herald Garter King of Arms is responsible for the coats of arms of Knights of the Garter and for all the elaborate ceremonial of the Order. Clarenceaux King of Arms is responsible for granting arms in the area south of the River Trent. Norroy and Ulster King of Arms is responsible for arms north of the Trent and in Ulster. The separate office of Ulster King of Arms was incorporated with Norroy King of Arms in 1943. There are six heralds – York, Chester, Windsor, Richmond, Somerset, and Lancaster – whose names indicate the areas and families their predecessors worked for. Finally there are four pursuivants (pronounced persevants). Their titles seem unlikely but in fact make perfect sense within the conventions of heraldry. They are Rouge Croix (the red cross of St George, patron saint of England and of the Order of the Garter), Blue Mantle (the colour of the Garter mantle), Portcullis (from the coat of arms of the Beaufort family from whom Henry VII was descended through his mother), and Rouge Dragon (red dragon, the symbol of Wales). These pursuivants were originally apprentices to the heralds proper. On some occasions additional heralds, who are not part of the College of Arms, may be appointed. These are called Heralds Extra-Ordinary.

The College of Arms is a part of the Royal Household and it is presided over by the Earl Marshal of England. Heralds are appointed by the Queen but the person who nominates new appointments for the Queen's official approval is the Earl Marshal.

Because even today prestige and honour are important to both individuals and corporate bodies, they like to have a tangible sign of it. The heralds are therefore kept busy designing the 200 or so new coats of arms which are granted each year by the Kings of Arms by the power vested in them by their Royal Charter. They also advise on genealogical and ceremonial matters and keep a record of all the coats of arms. For the devising and granting of new coats of arms and for their advice the heralds make their own charges. This is an essential privilege since from the Sovereign the Kings of Arms receive a yearly salary of twenty-three guineas (£24.15) and the heralds a mere seventeen guineas (£17.85).

The thirteen officers of arms take it in turns to be on duty. The herald on duty is known as the officer-in-waiting, and his personal banner hangs that day in the courtyard of the College of Arms. Although the officer-in-waiting is available to answer queries on all matters to do with heraldry and precedence the heralds are no longer required, as they once were, to tour the country checking that coats of arms were being used only by those truly entitled to them. When there was very little literacy and signs alone were widely used to convey people's intentions (shops for example were identified by their emblem rather than their name) to carry arms to which you were not entitled was tantamount to making a false declaration in order to claim land or property. Any disputes raised by these Visitations were investigated by the Court of Claims, presided over by the Earl Marshal himself. This Court dates back to the late fifteenth century but it is a long time since it has been required to settle disputes over coats of arms. However, as mentioned on p. 21, before the Coronation in 1953 a Commission of the Privy Council sitting as the Court of Claims sat to judge the claims of those who believed they had herditary rights to perform certain ceremonial functions at the Coronation itself. The large number of these claims is proof, if proof were needed, of how greatly honours from the Crown are valued.

The Earl Marshal of England is responsible for planning all the State ceremonies in England and Wales (in Scotland this is the responsibility of the Lord Lyon King of Arms). It is one of the heralds' main functions to assist him in this and to take part in most of the ceremonies. For some of these ceremonies there is a fee but such fees are purely nominal and the heralds perform their function for the honour alone. Since the men who become heralds are passionately devoted to their subject and to the ceremonial structure of which they form a part this is probably no great hardship. Nonetheless they may occasionally wish that, like their Scottish equivalents, they were fully paid up members of the civil service!

Ceremonies attended by the heralds include Coronations, the State Opening of Parliament, the Investiture of the Prince of Wales, the Procession for the Garter service, State funerals, Jubilee services, and Proclamations.

Garter King of Arms has some additional duties. He not only organizes the ceremonies of the Order of the Garter but is also responsible for the introduction of new peers into the House of Lords. Until the seventeenth century new peers were introduced directly to the Sovereign who invested them with their robes and insignia. Garter King of Arms then made a Proclamation of the style and title of the new peer for which he received a substantial fee. Later Garter King of Arms would introduce the same peer into the House of Lords and for his pains would receive the clothes the peer discarded in order to put on his peer's robes. James I sold so many new peerages in order to raise money that individual investiture became a chore. Instead peers were introduced directly to the House of Lords. The same procedure is followed today. So many new peers are now created that although it is officially the job of Garter King of Arms to introduce them he in his turn delegates wherever possible to one of the other heralds, for this is one of those ceremonial tasks for which there is no fee.

For their introduction new peers wear their robes (usually hired) and black cocked hats. Women do not have to remove their hats but men carry theirs. The new peer, preceded by Black Rod and Garter King of Arms or his substitute, goes down on one knee before the Lord Chancellor and presents his Writ of Summons. He then proffers his Letters Patent, which have been handed to him by Garter King of Arms, and when the Lord Chancellor has signified his acceptance they are handed to the Reading Clerk. The Reading Clerk reads out both the Writ of Summons and the Letters Patent, after which the peer takes the Oath of Allegiance and signs the Peers' Roll. The new peer and the two sponsors then take a seat and are instructed by Garter King of Arms to rise, take off their hats, and bow three times. After all this the new peer leaves the chamber, pausing on the way to shake hands with the Lord Chancellor.

The heralds have a special costume which they wear on all ceremonial occasions. The magnificently embroidered medieval style tabard which make them easily recognizable among all the other ceremonial uniforms and costumes is a fifteenth-century garment. It is derived from the long surcoats worn by knights over their chain mail. Since in their ceremonial duties the officers of arms are part of the Royal Household these tabards are embroidered with the royal coat of arms. They are distinguished by the material from which they are made; velvet for the Kings of Arms, satin for the heralds, and damask silk for the pursuivants. When the pursuivants were regarded more as apprentices than fully trained heralds they wore their tabards 'athwart', with the short sleeve pieces over chest and back and the long panels at the sides. This practice was discontinued in the seventeenth century and nowadays the title pursuivant is merely an historic one, all the officers of arms being equally well versed in their art.

A seventeenth-century herald in his splendid costume. Drawing by Sir Peter Lely

Underneath the tabards, the officers of arms wear a Victorian style military uniform dating from 1831. It consists of gold embroidered scarlet jacket (the tails of which are pinned up when the tabard is worn), black knee breeches, and black silver-buckled shoes. With this is worn a court sword and a cocked hat with ostrich feathers, white for a King of Arms and black for the others. A black velvet cap is worn for the Garter service. As a further symbol of their office they carry white staves surmounted with a dove or martlet. This is a symbol of their association with royal power. A similar stave or rod is carried by the great officers of State including the Earl Marshal. When the Sovereign dies or for some reason an officer leaves his post this stave is ceremonially broken over the knee to signify that the exercise of power on behalf of the Crown is now at an end.

At a coronation the dress is varied slightly. The breeches and stockings are white and the shoes have gold buckles. The Kings of Arms wear crowns which, like the peers, they place on their heads at the moment the Sovereign is crowned. The Coronation is also one of several occasions when the officers of arms, except the pursuivants, wear the collar of S's. This is a great honour, shared with the Lord Mayor of London and the Lords Chief Justice. The S is thought to stand for the Latin word *Seneschallus* meaning a Steward. Lord Lyon King of Arms in Scotland probably derived his office from the ancient office of king's shennachy, which has the same origin.

Despite their humble origins as administrators of tournaments the heralds today have become one of the most picturesque elements in much of Britain's State ceremonial. The part they take, despite the superficial glamour of their costume and insignia, is really very much like their original task, to make sure those who are also taking part in the ceremonial do the right thing at the right time.

The Orders of Chivalry

The Queen presides as Sovereign Head over the nine British Orders of Chivalry. In order of their foundation these are:

The Most Noble Order of the Garter (1348)
The Most Ancient and Most Noble Order of the Thistle (1702)
The Most Honourable Order of the Bath (1725)
The Most Illustrious Order of St Patrick (1783)
The Most Distinguished Order of St Michael and St George (1818)
The Most Exalted Order of the Star of India (1861)
The Most Eminent Order of the Indian Empire (1877)
The Royal Victorian Order (1896)
The Most Excellent Order of the British Empire (1917)

The Order of St Patrick and the two Indian Orders have been in abeyance since the independence of Eire in 1922 and of India in 1947.

Anyone familiar with the legends of King Arthur and the Knights of the Round Table knows that the idea of a noble brotherhood of knights exemplifying the chivalric ideals of Christian faith, courage, and courtliness goes back many hundreds of years, probably even before the Norman Conquest of 1066. Such ideals may seem rather outmoded in the twentieth century but people still seem eager to accept the public honour of belonging to one of the Orders of Chivalry. Many more, and wider ranging forms of public service than going into battle are now rewarded, but it is through the old-established system that honours are still bestowed and are generally more valued because of their links with the past. The vivid spectacle of some of the ceremonies, which persist from the time when the earlier Orders of Chivalry were founded, also adds to their mystique and offers further opportunities to see the type of ceremonial at which Britain excels.

The largest Order of Chivalry, the Order of the British Empire, has several ranks below knighthood of course, but it is through this and the other Orders that the Queen confers the rank and privilege of knighthood and it is with this rank that most of the ceremonial is associated.

There were two clear-cut methods of attaining a knighthood in medieval times. The first was based on the feudal system which meant in theory, if not always in practice, that all land ultimately belonged to the king and was parcelled out by him in return for service, usually military service. So the king could call on the service of knights who owed their allegiance directly to him and owned their land directly from him. This system was

Richard II knighting
Henry of Monmouth in
Ireland. From a fourteenth-
century manuscript

then repeated down the line so that large landowners then sub-divided their land in turn to tenants who repaid them by service.

The second way to become a fully fledged knight was to win your spurs on the field for conspicuous bravery or service to your lord. Depending on the circumstances such Knights Bachelor were also known as Knights of the Sword or Knights Banneret, and were held in special esteem.

There was also a nebulous but firmly rooted ideal of Knighthood and this is what still captures the imagination today. It was the romantic notion of adherence to a rigid code of chivalry with all that it implied in terms of courage, moral code, and courtly manners. A true knight of this type usually dedicated his service to a lady, and a famous one of his kind is Chaucer's 'veray parfit gentil knight'.

The customary method of attaining knighthood, which was bound up with the idea of land in repayment for service, was for a young boy of gentle birth to be sent at around the age of eight to a similar household to be trained. This practice could be regarded as the origin of modern boarding schools. At the new household the boy was taught the practical skills of riding, swordsmanship and so on which he would need, and he also absorbed the code of chivalry on which the lifestyle of his peers was based. At around the age of fifteen he would become an esquire (from the Latin word *scutarius* – a shield bearer) to an established knight. Finally, around the age of twenty he was ready to become a knight in his own right. A man who achieved his status of Knight Bachelor by this established route was sometimes called a Knight of the Bath.

This was because part of the initiation ceremony included the taking of a ritual bath, an event which had a certain rarity value even up to the present century. Like so much of our royal and national ceremonial the creation of a Knight Bachelor, like the investiture and installation of a knight of one of the Orders of Chivalry today, is steeped in Christian symbolism and ceremony. The evening before he was knighted the young man was shaved, had his hair cut, and took a bath to symbolize the purity with which he intended to enter his new rank. Then, simply dressed, he kept vigil all night in the chapel and at daybreak made his confession and heard mass.

After resting the new knight was taken into the presence of the person, usually the king, who was knighting him. There his golden spurs were placed on his feet by the two most noble knights present. His sword was then buckled on by the king who gave him the accolade (from the Latin *ad collum* – to the neck) of knighthood by tapping him lightly on the shoulder or neck and saying 'be thou a good knight'. The new knight then returned to the chapel to place his sword at the service of the Church. An episode followed which is amusing to us today but was taken seriously at the time. As the knight left the chapel he was accosted by the King's master

The Knights of the Bath
leaving Westminster
Abbey, 1749. Painting by
Canaletto

cook wielding a meat cleaver. The cook threatened to strike his newly won spurs from his heels if he ever proved an unworthy knight. This ritual continued long after the middle ages. In the eighteenth-century painting by Canaletto of the Knights of the Bath leaving Westminster Abbey, the cook and his cleaver are clearly visible.

Some of these attractive anachronisms have disappeared over the centuries but the ceremonial of the Orders of Chivalry is still based on the traditions of the early Knights Bachelor.

Of the three Orders of Chivalry which are most associated with pageantry and ritual, the Garter, Thistle, and Bath, the first two are in the Queen's personal gift. So too is the Royal Victorian Order, founded in 1896 by Queen Victoria to reward personal service to the Sovereign or members of the Royal Family. Unlike the others this Order has no installation service. The remaining Orders, and in particular The Most Excellent Order of the British Empire, are given as rewards for service and those who receive them in the Civil Division do so at the discretion of the Prime Minister, and in the Military Division at the discretion of the Sovereign (though *all* lists have to be approved by the Sovereign).

The Garter is the oldest Order of Chivalry, not just in Britain but also in Europe. It sets the pattern for the others in its ceremonial, its officers, and its insignia.

The Order was founded by Edward III, probably in 1348, following his victory over the French at Crécy in 1346. At a time when the hold of feudalism was weakening Edward III probably hoped that a new Order of Chivalry, inspired by the old legends of King Arthur and his Knights of the Round Table, would ensure the personal allegiance to him of an elite military group on which he could really depend. Nowadays, when ceremonies such as the Investiture of the Prince of Wales have been criticized for being contrived and unconvincing parodies of older rituals, it is interesting to note that our oldest Order of Chivalry was based 600 years ago on an improbable legend and an unspecified ritual. The patron saints of the new Order were St George, the patron saint of England, and St Edward the Confessor, the patron saint of English kings. Edward's original intention had been to call the Order the Company of St George. Before this was settled upon the incident occurred which according to tradition led to the Order being called the Garter. At a ball held after the capture of Calais in 1347 Joan, the Fair Maid of Kent, at that time wife of the Earl of Salisbury and later of the Black Prince, let her garter fall to the floor while dancing. When the courtiers laughed, the King, to distract attention from her embarrassment, picked it up and tied it round his own leg with the words *'Honi soi qui mal y pense'* – 'Shame on him who thinks evil of it'. It makes an attractive story and whether or not it is true in every

Two Princes of Wales in their garter robes. Edward the Black Prince became the second Prince of Wales in 1343 and the future Edward VIII was invested in 1911

detail (the tale was first told in Tudor times) there is no doubt that those words became the motto of the Order. A dark blue velvet *garter* edged with gold and with the motto embroidered onto it in gold thread is part of the insignia. The rest of the insignia are:

Mantle Dark blue velvet lined with white taffeta. The Star of the Order is embroidered on the left breast of the Sovereign's mantle where the Knights have the Arms of the Order, Argent a Cross Gules (for St George) encircled by the garter.

Hood Crimson velvet: the vestige of this is worn fastened to the Mantle and over the right shoulder.

Hat Black velvet, Tudor style, with a large plume of white ostrich feathers.

Collar Formed of 26 buckled garters in gold surrounding Tudor roses of enamel and alternating with knots of gold cord.

George Gold and enamel pendant representing St George and the dragon. This hangs from the collar on collar days.

Badge or *Lesser George* Represents St George and the dragon. Fastens the riband at the right hip.

Star Within its radiations this contains the cross of St George surrounded by an enamel garter, the points or rays in silver. Worn on the left breast on full dress uniform, court dress, morning coat, full evening dress coat, and dinner jacket.

Riband Blue, worn over the left shoulder and fastened at the right hip by the *Lesser George*. This manner of wearing it was introduced by Charles II who took a great interest in the Order.

The Officers of the Order are now six:

The Prelate (The Bishop of Winchester *ex officio*)
The Chancellor
The Register (Dean of Windsor)
Garter King of Arms
The Gentleman Usher of the Black Rod
The Secretary

The Order consists of the Sovereign as Head of the Order, the Prince of Wales as a constituent member of the Order and twenty-four Knights Companion. There is also a varying, though small, number of 'Stranger Knights', which enables the Queen to offer the Garter as a mark of special esteem to foreign sovereigns and princes.

In 1910 Edward VII revived the practice of appointing Ladies of the Order. These are members of the Royal Family or, like the Queen of Denmark, of royal birth. In addition, linked with the Order, there are thirteen Military Knights of Windsor, whose bright scarlet coats and white sashes add to the pageantry on ceremonial occasions. These twenty-six were originally known as the 'Poor Knights of Windsor', but in 1833 William IV gave them the more dignified title they enjoy today. They were intended by Edward to be chosen from men of gentle birth, veteran Knights who had fallen on hard times after giving good service to their country. In addition to attending the Knights Companion they had also to represent them at the daily church services which were part of the constitution of the Order. Today they are retired officers who lodge at Windsor Castle and who still attend the daily services and take part in the ceremonial of the Order. It is also their duty to Keep a Watch over the coffin before a Royal funeral at the Castle.

The chapel of the Order is St George's Chapel in the precincts of Windsor Castle. This chapel was rebuilt in the reign of Edward IV in the fifteenth century, and is considered one of the finest examples of late Gothic architecture in Europe. The chapel is lined with wooden stalls, one for each of the Knights Companion of the Order of the Garter. Above each stall is a helm with a carved crest and a banner of the Arms of its present occupant. On the wall at the back of each stall are several brass or enamelled plates, called Garter Stall Plates, which commemorate by his coat of arms each of the knights who was formerly entitled to a stall. The earliest go back to the fifteenth century.

The investiture of a Knight of the Garter is the ceremony on which the ceremonies of the other Orders are based. Although it takes place in private in the Throne Room of Windsor Castle, a knowledge of what has taken place in the morning makes the afternoon procession to the chapel for the Installation Service a much more interesting and rewarding experience for those who have come to see it. On the morning of the annual Garter Chapter and Service the Officers and Knights Companion gather in the Throne Room at the Castle. The steps to the Throne are carpeted in blue, the colour of the Garter, and the sense of pageantry is enhanced by the Queen's Bodyguard of the Yeomen of the Guard in their Tudor costume, who are posted round the walls. When the Queen, who is usually accompanied by the Duke of Edinburgh, the Queen Mother, and the Prince of Wales, is seated Garter King of Arms and Black Rod go to fetch the Knight Elect. He is brought between two knight sponsors to the Sovereign who personally invests him with all the insignia of the Order. First is the Garter which is symbolically circled round the left leg and held there by Garter King of Arms while the following admonition is read out:

To the honour of God Omnipotent and in Memorial of the Blessed Martyr, St George, tie about thy leg, for thy renown, this most Noble Garter. Wear it as a symbol of the Most Illustrious Order, never to be forgotten or laid aside, that thereby thou mayest be admonished to be courageous, and having undertaken a just war, with which thou

shalt be engaged, thou mayest stand firm, valiantly fight, courageously and successfully conquer.

Paradoxically Ladies of the Order have always worn the Garter on the left arm and not on the leg. Last of all the Prelate administers the oath of the Order. The investiture ceremony is followed by lunch for the knights, their spouses and the Officers of the Order in the Waterloo Chamber. This magnificent banqueting hall was built at the instigation of George IV to commemorate the allied victory over Napoleon at Waterloo.

After this lunch, at about 2.30 p.m. the Procession lines up in St George's Hall to walk from the royal apartments to the Chapel at the foot of the hill. The first part of the Procession is headed by the Constable and Governor of Windsor Castle, and the Military Knights of Windsor in their scarlet uniforms. Next are the heralds and pursuivants of the College of Arms, splendid in their tabards with the Royal Arms richly embroidered in bright shades of red, blue, and gold. Behind the heralds come the Knights of the Garter themselves, creating an unforgettable spectacle in their full blue mantles and the Tudor bonnets with their generous ostrich plumes and wearing their Collars of the Order. After them come Princes of the Blood and the Queen Mother. And finally come the Officers of the Order leading the Sovereign's Procession, which includes Garter King of Arms and the Gentleman Usher of the Black Rod. Next are the Sovereign and Consort who have the trains of their mantles held up by pages in scarlet livery. Bringing up the rear of the whole Procession are the Queen's Bodyguard of the Yeomen of the Guard.

In addition to the splendour of the Procession itself the festival atmosphere is enhanced by the music of two military bands and the route to St George's Chapel is lined with soldiers of the Household Cavalry, this being one of the few occasions when they parade dismounted. We owe this opportunity to see Windsor Castle being used for an event which does justice to the magnificence of the setting to George VI. It was he who reinstituted the Procession in 1948 after a lapse of 103 years.

At the Chapel the Procession is met by the Clergy, Canons and others of the College of St George. This group, headed by the Sacristans and the

Cross Bearer, proceeds into the Chapel and a trumpet fanfare sounds as the Queen enters by the West Door. If a new knight has been invested that morning he is led to his stall by the Garter King of Arms while the Chancellor calls out his name. There then follows a simple service. Afterwards the Queen and other members of the Royal Family return to the Castle in carriages and the rest of the participants are taken back by car.

Date **The Garter Service, or Service of Thanksgiving (and the preceding Procession through the precincts of Windsor Castle) is held in June every year, normally on the Monday before the opening of the Royal Ascot Race Meeting (usually the third week in June). This is the date closest to St George's Day, 23 April, when the Queen is sure to be at Windsor as she is always in residence to attend Ascot.**
Place **St George's Chapel, Windsor and precincts of Windsor Castle.**
Time **2.30 p.m.**
How to attend **It is not possible for members of the public to witness the Investiture ceremony in the Throne Room. However this and the other State Rooms are open to the public on most days.**

The service is not open to the public, and admission to view the Procession is by ticket only. Anyone is eligible but tickets are issued on a first-come-first-served basis and are limited. It is therefore essential to make an application in writing, enclosing a stamped, addressed envelope, at the beginning of January **(see p. 176).**

THE MOST ANCIENT AND MOST NOBLE ORDER OF THE THISTLE

This Order of Chivalry is generally accounted the Scottish equivalent of the Garter. Its motto is *'Nemo Me Impune Lacessit'* – 'No one Provokes Me with Impunity'. The Order is not as ancient as its full title seems to suggest. There are references to Knights of the Thistle as far back as the early fifteenth century and it can certainly be traced back to 1540 when James V of Scotland created the Order of St Andrew. This consisted of the king and twelve Knights Companion, the symbolism being of course the traditional idea of Christ and his twelve apostles. This Order lapsed, being regarded as too Catholic in its concept by the Reformation Church.

In 1687 the Catholic James II (James VII of Scotland) founded the Order of the Thistle dedicated to St Andrew, which was clearly based on

The Procession of the Knights of the Garter in 1576. Etching by Marcus Gheeraerts I the 1540 Order of St Andrew while the title was a century older. The King himself relished the notion that the real origins of the Order went back to about AD 800 when the Scots King Achaius defeated the English Saxon ruler Athelstan and instituted a brotherhood of twelve knights to commemorate the victory.

James's enforced abdication in 1689 prevented the Order being formally recognized and it was his daughter, Queen Anne, who revived it properly by the issue of a Royal Warrant on 31 December 1702. However, the number of knights remained at eight, as it had been in her father's time. It was not until 1821, when George IV made the first visit by a reigning monarch to Scotland since James II, that the numbers were increased. Today the Order consists of the Sovereign, Royal Knights, Extra Knights (usually foreign royalty), and sixteen Knights Companion. The Insigia of the Order are:

Surcoat Dark blue velvet lined with white taffeta.

Mantle Dark green velvet lined with white taffeta. A large Star of the Order is embroidered on the left shoulder.

Hood Dark green velvet lined with white taffeta, attached to right shoulder of the mantle.

Hat Black velvet Tudor bonnet with white plume.

Collar Gold and enamel with alternating devices of thistles and sprigs of rue.

Badge Depicts St Andrew in gold, carrying a white enamelled St Andrew's cross, surrounded by gold rays.

Star A white enamelled cross of St Andrew with a green enamelled thistle at the centre surrounded by the motto. Gold rays radiate from the cross.

Riband Dark green, worn in the Garter fashion over the left shoulder, fastened by the badge on the right hip.

The Officers of the Order are:

The Sovereign
The Dean of St Giles
The Chancellor
The Lord Lyon King of Arms
The Gentleman Usher of the Green Rod

The chapel at Holyroodhouse was designated by James II and VII (of Scotland) as the chapel of the Order, but it was destroyed in the 1688 uprising. The knights now use a small gem of a chapel designed by Sir Robert Mortimer, which was added to the cathedral of St Giles in 1910/11. Because it was built specifically for the Order its decoration is symbolic, incorporating the shields of the original knights, images of St Andrew, and the predominating theme of the Thistle. It is in the Gothic style of the late fifteenth century with a brightly coloured roof and stalls for the individual knights like those for the Knights of the Garter in St George's Chapel, Windsor. Because the chapel is so small there is not room to hang the banners over the stalls but commemorative stall plates are fixed on the back of the stalls as they are for past Knights of the Garter. The banners are hung in the Preston aisle of the cathedral itself. The Queen's great grandfather, Edward VII, took a keen personal interest in the design and construction of the chapel while he was Sovereign of the Order.

Each year there is a service for the Order held in the chapel which may be on St Andrew's Day, 30 November, or an adjacent Sunday, although the date is flexible.

If a new knight is to be installed there is sometimes a separate Installation Service held on a date when the Queen is in Scotland. This is preceded by an Investiture based on the Garter Investiture. The people who congregate in Parliament Square outside the cathedral before and after a Thistle service are rewarded by a sight similar to the Procession of the Knights of the Garter to St George's Chapel at Windsor.

The Knights of the Thistle, seen recently on their way to St Giles's Cathedral

The Knights Companion, the Lord Lyon King of Arms, three heralds, three pursuivants, and the Usher of the Green Rod robe in the Library of the Writers to Her Majesty's Signet, across the square from the cathedral. The Queen and members of the royal party drive from Holyroodhouse to join those waiting at the Signet Library. They are met by a Guard of Honour of the Royal Company of Archers as they arrive at the Library. A Procession is then formed headed by the heralds and pursuivants, the Lord Lyon King of Arms and the Dean of the Thistle, followed by Knights of the Thistle, and finally the Queen and the royal party. The Procession crosses the square and walks through the cathedral, which is lined with men of the Royal Company of Archers, to the Thistle Chapel. In front of the Sovereign walks the senior Scottish Earl present carrying the Sword of State which has been brought from Edinburgh Castle under its own armed escort. As the Queen enters the cathedral a fanfare is sounded by Her Majesty's Household Trumpeters, and hymns are sung as the Procession makes its way to the chapel. In the chapel the new knight is taken before the Queen, then conducted by the Lord Lyon King of Arms to his stall where the oath is administered by the Dean. Finally the Lord Lyon King of Arms reads out the style and titles of the new knight. A short service in the chapel is then usually followed by another in the main body of the cathedral after which the Procession reforms and returns to the Signet Library.

Place **St Giles's Cathedral, Edinburgh.**
Date **The annual service and Installation Service are often combined. There is no longer a set date for the service. If the Queen is to attend it will be arranged to accommodate her schedule. See the Press for details.**
Time **The service begins at 11.30 a.m. and lasts until approximately 12. 40 p.m.**

The Procession from the Signet Library across Parliament Square to the cathedral begins at approximately 11.00 a.m. Important guests may begin to arrive at the cathedral about half an hour beforehand. Members of the public who wish to see the Procession should arrive early, about 9.00 a.m.
Tickets: **There is very limited seating inside the cathedral for the service. Tickets are issued at the discretion of the Dean of St Giles (see p. 176).**

THE MOST HONOURABLE ORDER OF THE BATH

The name of this Order might be confusing since all medieval knights not created on the field of battle became knights bachelor after a lengthy period of training and an elaborate ceremonial which included a bath taken as a symbol of spiritual purification (see p. 103). However, the Order was not created until 1725 when George I issued Letters Patent which brought it into being. The actual wording spoke of the Order being 'revived' and this has given rise to several theories as to its true origins. The most convincing of these is that the idea goes back to the Coronation of Henry IV in 1399. As was the custom he spent the eve of his Coronation at the Tower of London and that very day created a large number of new Knights Bachelor who, because they all went through the ceremonial together, became known as the Knights of the Bath. These knights, although they did not belong to an Order, had a certain amount of prestige because of the timing and manner of their creation. Succeeding monarchs followed Henry IV's example of creating knights on the eve of their coronation and the exclusiveness of this group was further emphasized by the fact that they wore distinctive crimson robes at coronations similar to the later crimson mantle of the Order when it was ultimately created. The last monarch to spend the eve of his Coronation at the Tower and create such a group of knights was Charles II in 1660.

When George I established the Order of the Bath it was intended to be a military order of thirty-six Knights Companion created from those officers of the Army and Navy who had performed especially distinguished service. However, after the victory of the battle of Waterloo in 1815 the Prince Regent felt that so many military men should be rewarded for their service that the Order was extended to three different ranks – Knights Grand Cross, Knights Commander, and Companions. In this the Order differs from the Garter and Thistle which have only one class, Knights Companion. The name was also changed on this occasion to its present name of The Most Honourable Order of the Bath. In 1847 Queen Victoria made further changes so that the Order became open to civilians.

The motto of the Order of the Bath is *'Tria Juncta in Uno'* – 'Three joined in One', a reference to the Trinity and to the three kingdoms of England, Scotland and France or Ireland. The Insignia of the Order are:

Mantle Dark crimson satin lined with white taffeta. An embroidered Star of the Order on the left shoulder. (Knights Grand Cross only.)
Collar Gold and enamel made up of imperial crowns, roses, thistles, shamrocks, and white enamelled knots. (Knights Grand Cross only.)
Badge (Military) For collars and neck insignia. Three crowns surrounded by the motto. This central device is surrounded by a laurel wreath of of green enamel and placed upon a white Maltese Cross with gold balls at each of the eight points.
Badge (Civil) For collars and neck insignia. A shamrock, thistle, and rose about a sceptre between three crowns surrounded by a band bearing the motto of the Order, gold throughout.
The badge is worn suspended from the collar or the sash. Those classes not entitled to wear a collar wear the badge suspended from a crimson riband at the neck.

Star (*Military*) A Star with silver streamers on which is imposed a gold Maltese cross with three crowns surrounded by the motto and laurel wreath.
Star (*Civil*) Eight-pointed star. Three crowns in the centre surrounded by the motto.
Riband Crimson silk, worn over right shoulder and with the Badge suspended on the left hip.

Under the Sovereign and the Great Master the Officers of the Order are:

The Dean of the Order (at present the Dean of Westminster)
Bath King of Arms
The Registrar and Secretary
The Genealogist
The Gentleman Usher of the Scarlet Rod
The Deputy Secretary

The chapel of the Order is the beautiful Henry VII Chapel in Westminster Abbey which is particularly remarkable for its fine ceiling. Here the senior members of the Order, the Knights Grand Cross, have their banners hung above and commemorative stall plates fixed to the back of their stalls, just as the Knights of the Garter and the Thistle have in their chapels. As there are well over 100 Knights Grand Cross there are not enough stalls for all at once and the stalls are allocated in order of seniority.

George V in 1913 revived the Installation Ceremony which had not been held since 1812. This is normally held in the chapel of the Order every

Ceremonial at a Banquet of the Knights of the Bath in Westminster Hall in 1689. 'Bath King at Arms proclaiming the Style of Prince William, at the bringing in of the Second Course, attended by Heralds and Pursuivants.'

four years. The Knights Grand Cross process to the chapel where those to
be installed each swear an oath of loyalty and are then placed in a stall by
the Great Master. At present the Great Master is Prince Charles. The
Queen is not present at every Installation Ceremony of the Order of the
Bath but did attend in 1975 when Prince Charles was installed as Great
Master.

Date **The Installation Service takes place about once every four years. It will not take
place again until 1986.**
Time **Service begins 11.15 a.m.**
Place **Westminster Abbey.**
**Although this is not a private ceremony priority is given to Members of the Order and
their guests. Application by members of the public for tickets can be made (see p. 176).**

THE MOST DISTINGUISHED ORDER OF ST MICHAEL AND ST GEORGE
THE ORDER OF ST JOHN

There are two other ceremonies which are of interest, and which are sometimes, though not necessarily always, royal occasions. First is the Service
for the Most Distinguished Order of St Michael and St George (founded
1818 and almost exclusively used to honour members of the foreign service).
This takes place every year in the Order's chapel in St Paul's Cathedral. At
the service the banners of the Knights and Dames Grand Cross are carried
by friends or relatives.

The Duke of Kent kisses
the Queen's hand as she
arrives at St Paul's
Cathedral for the service
of St Michael and St
George, 1976

The other ceremony is the annual commemoration service in St Paul's Cathedral of the Order of St John. This is not an Order of Chivalry but it has many historic associations and the Queen is Sovereign Head of the Order which is largely concerned with maintaining the St John Ambulance Service and the Opthalmic Hospital in Jerusalem. The Grand Prior of the Order is the Duke of Gloucester. The annual service attended by the Grand Prior and the Lord Mayor is a wonderful spectacle which combines the pageantry both of chivalry and of the City of London. It is the more impressive because the Order of St John is not an attractive anachronism but a society which performs an essential task in our modern society.

Place **The commemoration service is usually held in St Paul's Cathedral.**
Tickets **Attendance at the service is only open to members of the Order of St John. Details of dates and times for those who wish to see the arrival of the Grand Prior, Lord Mayor, and other distinguished guests can be obtained by reading the Court and Social pages of 'The Times' or 'Daily Telegraph' or telephoning the Order's Offices, 01-253 6644.**

Conferment of Honours

The names of those who are honoured are, with the occasional exception of the Garter, Thistle, Royal Victorian Order, and Order of Merit which are in the Queen's personal gift, announced in the Press twice a year. These are the New Year's Honours List, and the Birthday Honours List which is issued on the Queen's official birthday. These lists are compiled from names put forward to the Prime Minister's office, mainly by large official groups such as the Civil Service and the armed forces but also by smaller groups and even by individuals. From all the names submitted about 4,000 people are chosen every year. Each of these is sent a letter from the Prime Minister's office saying that the Prime Minister intends to submit his or her name to the Queen for an Honour and wishes to know whether this will be acceptable. The Honour itself is not offered directly so no one can say they turned down an Honour from the Queen. In the event very few people object to having their names submitted although it is occasionally thought that people decline in the hope that they may be offered something slightly more impressive next time around. After writing back to accept, nothing more happens until the recipient sees his or her name in the published list.

The Order of Chivalry which accounts for most of the Honours is the Most Excellent Order of the British Empire. This was founded by George V in 1917 during the First World War to reward civilians for special service to the Empire. The motto of the Order is 'For God and the Empire'. In the following year it was extended to include military personnel as well. Since the Order is open to civilians and the military, men and women, and has five classes which allow for distinction between different levels and types of service and achievement, the Order of the British Empire is an ideal channel for rewarding merit in almost every sphere. It is perhaps a pity that its title has not been altered slightly to encompass the Commonwealth as well as the rather archaic sounding Empire as from time to time it is turned down as a matter of principle by foreigners whom the government would like to honour. The Queen is Sovereign Head of the Order and the five classes are:

Knights and Dames Grand Cross (G B E)
Knights and Dames Commander (K B E and D B E)
Commanders (C B E)
Officer (O B E)
Members, Fourth and Fifth Class (M B E)

The chapel of the Order is in St Paul's Cathedral, the only church large enough to hold even a fraction of the 100,000 or so people belonging to the Order. Although a service is held every three or four years, there is no special Installation Service for knights of the type performed for the Garter and Thistle. Nor is there a private Investiture Service for knights.

After the Honours Lists have been published invitations are sent out to attend one of the dozen or so Investitures which are held throughout the year. Each person being honoured is allowed to bring two guests. By holding so many Investitures the Queen tries as far as possible to award every Honour herself from the Knighthoods to the M B Es. When she is unavoidably absent, on a foreign tour for example, another member of the Royal Family deputizes for her. On occasion an Investiture is held in Edinburgh and the Queen sometimes holds Investitures personally when travelling abroad.

Investitures in London are held in the ballroom at Buckingham Palace. Guests sit on tiered seats along the walls and those who are to be honoured sit on small gilt chairs in the centre of the room. At one end of the room a military orchestra plays selections of popular tunes which are sometimes chosen, it is said, to compliment the person at that moment speaking to the Queen. An Australian friend receiving the C B E was pleasantly surprised to hear the strains of 'Waltzing Matilda'! At the other end of the room is the dais on which stands the Queen's throne. At the back of the dais stand five Yeomen of the Guard who add colour to the occasion, and two Gurkha

Orderly Officers. It was Edward VII who first specified that the Sovereign
should be attended by Indian Army officers, and the present Queen who
specified the Gurkhas. The National Anthem is played and the Queen and
her party enter. The recipients are divided into groups and approach the
Queen from the left of the dais. As the Lord Chamberlain announces an
individual's name he or she bows or curtsies and then approaches to receive
the Honour and hear a few personal words spoken by the Queen.

Interestingly in spite of the numbers everyone comes away with the
feeling that their award was a very personal tribute indeed. The Queen's

The Queen knighting
Francis Chichester at
Greenwich in 1967 on his
return from his single-
handed voyage round the
world

relaxed attitude to the Investitures was evident when on one such occasion she delightedly announced the birth of her first grandson before proceeding with the business in hand. Those knights who are dubbed on these occasions rather than invested as members of the older Orders of Chivalry do actually kneel before the Queen and are tapped on the shoulder by the sword, a custom derived from the need to create knights quickly during a battle. Occasionally, as when the Queen knighted Sir Francis Chichester at Greenwich on his return from his single-handed world voyage, the venue and procedure for Investitures are varied.

Sometimes awards are made posthumously, often for acts of great courage and dedication to duty particularly now that terrorism has become a way of life. The Queen always presents such tributes in a private meeting with the person's family before the main Investiture ceremony begins.

There is undoubtedly a need for some means of recognizing courage, service, and achievement, especially when these are often found in the least financially rewarding occupations. It is difficult to imagine an alternative method to the present honours system, especially because the personal presentation by the Queen herself adds so greatly to the Honour or award itself.

(Full details of *all* the orders can be found in *Whitaker's Almanack*.)

The Investiture of the Prince of Wales

Wales has been formally united with England for far longer than Scotland. For hundreds of years the English kings tried to subdue both the Welsh and the Scots by military might but although this undoubtedly helped wear down their resistance unity with both countries eventually came fairly peacefully. The unification of Scotland and England in 1707 became possible because the two countries shared a Stuart monarch. Wales and England were formally united in the reign of Henry VIII by two statutes, one in 1532 and the other in 1536. This again was made easier because of the family connections of the monarch. Henry's father, Henry VII, was the founder of a dynasty bearing the Welsh name of Tudor. His grandmother, the widow of Henry V, had married a Welshman called Owen Tudor.

Henry VII followed tradition by creating his eldest son and heir Prince Arthur, Prince of Wales. When Prince Arthur died prematurely the next son, Henry, later Henry VIII, was created Prince of Wales in his turn. These Tudor Princes of Wales were probably the first imposed on the Welsh people by the English crown who were not totally unacceptable.

The first English Prince of Wales was the son of Edward I. Edward I was determined to crush resistance to English influence in Wales after the first Welsh Prince of Wales, Llewellyn ap Gryffyd, led a rebellion against him which broke the terms of an earlier agreement made between the two men. After the Welshman's death in 1281 Edward's campaign continued to be successful and in 1284, while he was living at Caernarvon Castle in order to direct personally the subduing of the Welsh, his son Edward was born. Tradition has it that almost immediately he presented the new infant to the Welsh people from the battlements of the castle, saying, 'Here is your Prince who was born in Wales and speaks no word of English'. This was hardly surprising since the Prince could not speak at all! Whether or not that apocryphal story has any basis in truth there is no doubt that Edward, having rid himself of one troublesome native Prince of Wales, thought it wise to replace him with a prince of his own choosing. The boy was actually created Prince of Wales and Earl of Chester in 1301, by which time his elder brother had died and he was heir apparent. Since then it has been the custom to create the heir apparent Prince of Wales or, as in the case of George IV's daughter Charlotte, Princess of Wales.

However, this title and that of Earl of Chester which is given with it are not inherited directly, as are the heir's other titles Duke of Cornwall, Duke of Rothesay, Earl of Carrick, Baron Renfrew, Lord of the Isles, and Great Steward of Scotland. Each Prince of Wales has to be invested individually with the title and some heirs to the throne, such as Henry VIII's son Edward, were never given the title. There is no particular age specified for creating a Prince of Wales. The future George IV received the title five days after he was born in 1762. The present Prince of Wales was nine years old when to his great embarrassment he heard the news while sitting with friends at school watching the opening of the Commonwealth Games at Cardiff on television. The Queen, who could not be present in person because of a sinus operation, delivered a tape-recorded message in which she announced the creation of Prince Charles as Prince of Wales, and stated her intention of presenting him at Caernarvon when he was old enough.

The elaborate ceremony which accompanied the Investiture in 1969 of Prince Charles as Prince of Wales, and the fact that the ceremony took place at Caernarvon, birthplace of the first English Prince of Wales, led many people to believe that both ceremonial and setting were somehow laid down by tradition. In fact the only real necessity is that the Prince should receive the Letters Patent granting his new title, and that he should be formally introduced into the House of Lords.

However, earlier Princes of Wales were also created with considerably more than the bare minimum of ceremony. The manner of their investiture was laid down in the Charter by which Edward the Black Prince was created the second Prince of Wales by his father Edward III in 1343. This Charter was read out and the actions performed to suit the words. So the Prince was invested with the insignia as they were read out, 'with a coronet around his head (*per sertum in capite*), 'with a gold ring on his finger (*anulum in digitum aureum*), and with a silver rod (*virgam argenteam*). This last was a symbol of his princely power, just like the sceptre which is given to the king or queen when an English Sovereign is crowned. For centuries a wand, rod, or sceptre has been the symbol of royal power or permission to wield royal power. The Investiture of a Prince of Wales was, as originally laid down, slightly reminiscent of a coronation, which was fitting since it enhanced the dignity of Wales as a separate Principality. Yet the Investiture is also like the Investiture of any other title which owes its origin to the English Crown as the fount of honour.

So after receiving the wand as a symbol of his power the Prince had then to kneel and make the oath of allegiance like any other newly created peer.

In 1616, Prince Charles, son of James I, was invested as Prince of Wales in the customary fashion with a formal Investiture ceremony along the lines laid down for the Investiture of the Black Prince. After his investiture the newly invested Prince was shown his seat in the House of Lords. The similarity to a coronation is marked in the descriptions we have of several of these occasions, not just their form but the festivity which surrounded the event. This similarity was further enhanced by the custom of creating Knights of the Bath on the evening before the ceremony, just as was customary before the coronation of the monarch, and by the sumptuous banquet, like the traditional Coronation Banquet, which followed. No further Prince of Wales was created until a century later, when George I's son was given the title.

The Hanoverians had almost complete contempt for the manners and customs of their new kingdom. Lord Hervey, who chronicled in such detail the courts of the Hanoverians, wrote of George II: 'There was nothing English ever commended in his presence that he did not always show, or pretend to show, was surpassed by something of the same kind in Germany.' It may have been for this reason that, while continuing the tradition of granting the heir apparent the titles of Prince of Wales and Earl of Chester, all the ceremony previously associated with the Investiture was dropped. Instead the title was validated by the simple procedure of affixing the Great Seal to the Letters Patent of the Creation. In 1911 it was decided to restore the pageantry and the Investiture has become easily the most spectacular of the traditional ceremonies which have been re-introduced and revitalized in the twentieth century.

The Investiture of the Prince of Wales (later Edward VIII) in 1911 was the first such ceremony for almost exactly 300 years. It was intended, like the Investiture of Prince Charles in 1969, as a compliment to the Welsh and as a demonstration of Anglo-Welsh unity in the face of the growing demands of Welsh nationalism. Then as in 1969 it is hard to evaluate whether or not its effect was conciliatory or inflammatory. The 1911 Investiture was largely at the instigation of the eminent Welshman, David Lloyd George, who was Prime Minister during and immediately after the First World War. Because there was no recent precedent this Investiture was an amalgam of the Investiture ceremony laid down for the Black Prince with ritual reminiscent of a coronation. In addition to the coronet, ring, and wand (sceptre), which are themselves a part of the coronation ceremony of a Sovereign, there was also a mantle. The whole proceeding was rounded off by a religious service just as a coronation is integrated into a Communion service. Afterwards the Prince was presented to his people – not simply as the first Prince had been by his father but as the Sovereign to be crowned is presented to the people in the 'theatre' of Westminster Abbey.

The choice of Caernarvon Castle added a whole new dimension to the event. Although the story persists of Edward creating his son Prince of Wales immediately after his birth at Caernarvon Castle no Prince from that time until 1911 had ever been invested in Wales, let alone at the castle. Because the title of Prince of Wales was as much associated with the heir to the English throne as the Principality itself, the Investiture

Prince Edward (later Edward VIII) with his parents at his Investiture as Prince of Wales in 1911

had generally taken place at Westminster so that it could be followed by the introduction to the House of Lords. It is generally assumed that the choice of Caernarvon as the setting for the revival of the Investiture, rather than at Westminster where it had been customary, was the doing of Lloyd George. Not only did he have a strong sentimental streak but he was himself Constable of Caernarvon Castle as well as MP for Caernarvon and must have seen the occasion as an ideal opportunity for enhancing his own prestige.

Much of the procedure from 1911 formed the basis of the 1969 Investiture, including of course the venue. What did not warrant repetition was the somewhat ludicrous quasi-medieval costume, the 'preposterous rig' as the Prince himself called it which was devised as being suitable for an occasion with its roots so deep in the past. This had consisted of white breeches, white silk stockings and black pumps, with a richly embroidered purple velvet surcoat trimmed with ermine. Around his knee the Prince wore a Garter in the medieval fashion. George v was pleased with his son's appearance, 'The dear boy did it all remarkably well and looked so nice' he wrote in his diary. The Prince of Wales on the other hand later recollected that he was 'half fainting with heat and nervousness'. Prince Charles was spared the white satin knee breeches and chose to wear Naval uniform with both the collar and riband of the Garter. One of the innovations of the 1911 Investiture which was retained in 1969 was the Prince's reply in Welsh to the Loyal Address of the people of Wales. In 1911, coached by Mr Lloyd George, the Prince was able to say 'Diolch fy nghalon i Hen wlad nhadua' – 'Thanks from the depths of my heart to the ancient land of my fathers' – and 'Mor o gan yw Cymru i gyd' – 'All Wales is a sea of song'.

The Investiture of the Prince of Wales

Prince Charles kneeling before the Queen at his Investiture in 1969

Prince Charles, following a term at the University of Wales, was able to make his reply entirely in Welsh.

The Investiture of Prince Charles as Prince of Wales seems to have confirmed the value and validity of the 1911 revival and given the ceremony greater prominence than ever before. It seems likely that any future Prince (or indeed Princess) of Wales will be invested in the same way at the same place.

The new procedure has turned it into what it never was before – a Welsh occasion. Like the Coronation it has also become a major public spectacle and this too is reflected in the form the day takes. The tone was set by the clear awning which covered the dais in 1969, designed by Lord Snowdon to give everyone the best possible view. John Brooke-Little, one of the heralds present and involved in the planning, describes how the number of processions has increased from two, the King's and the Prince's, to about a dozen, so that the spectacle is greatly enhanced and a greater number of Welsh people involved. Those present now include the Archdruid of Wales and officers and members of the Gorseald of Bards, civic dignitaries from Welsh towns and from the capital, Cardiff, the High Sheriffs of the Welsh counties, Lords Lieutenant of the Welsh counties, Welsh Members of Parliament, and representatives of the Welsh churches.

The Processions enter through the Water Gate and the people forming them take their places behind the dais. The Prince of Wales arrives at 2.35 a.m. with an Escort of Household Cavalry. As he arrives his Banner is flown above the Castle. He then waits at the Chamberlain Tower until summoned. The Queen's Procession then arrives and the Prince of Wales's Banner is taken down while the Royal Banner is flown. Before proceeding to her place the Queen is presented with the key of the Castle by the Constable. She touches it and says 'Sir Constable, I return the key of this Castle into your keeping'.

When the Queen is seated on her throne on the dais Garter King of Arms is sent to fetch the Prince himself. He comes with his own Procession, preceded by the heralds and with two Welsh Lords on either side as his supporters. Four Lords then follow carrying the Princely insignia, the coronet, the rod, the ring, and the mantle. These are the Welsh equivalent of the Crown Jewels and the 1969 insignia like the 1911 insignia are now on display in Wales.

The Prince kneels before his Sovereign while his Letters Patent are read out in both English and Welsh. During the Welsh version the Queen invests the Prince with the ornaments referred to. Seeing parent and child together in this ancient ritual is an emotional moment. However, Noël Coward in his recently published diaries gives an insight into the very human nature of the two people performing that immensely symbolic ritual in 1969. 'I told the Queen how moved I had been by Prince Charles's

Investiture and she gaily shattered my sentimental illusions by saying that they were both struggling not to giggle, because at the dress rehearsal the crown was too big and extinguished him like a candle-snuffer!'

After the Investiture the Prince pays Homage to the Sovereign with the same words used to pay Homage at the Coronation.

'I, Charles, Prince of Wales, do become your liege man of life and limb and earthly worship, and faith and truth I will bear unto you to live and die against all manner of folks.'

The Sovereign and the Prince exchange the Kiss of Fealty and he then sits on the throne at her side. The Loyal Address from the people of Wales is read out, to which the Prince then makes his reply in Welsh. An ecumenical religious service follows.

The final part of the ceremony is the Presentations, an element which takes its inspiration from the presentation of the Sovereign at the Coronation and the supposed presentation of his son by Edward I in 1284. There are three presentations which take place to the fanfare of trumpets. The first is from the balcony above Queen Eleanor's Gate, named after the mother of the first English Prince of Wales. The second is from the King's Gate, and the last is from the steps between the two wards of the Castle. This done the Procession reforms and returns to the Eagle Tower. It then leaves the Castle and processes through the town to the assembly point.

It seems strange that it has taken nearly seven centuries to establish a formal structure for a ceremony which both in its venue and language emphasizes the Welshness of the Prince of Wales. The revival of a traditional investiture and the new life which has been breathed into this almost defunct ceremony in the twentieth century tells us something of the importance of ceremonial to the national consciousness and of the need which pomp and pageantry fulfil in all our lives.

Full details of a future Investiture would be in the local and national Press and available from tourist authorities, and there would certainly be an official programme on sale in advance throughout the country.

Royal Ceremonial in Scotland

Although the English and the Scots have been united under the same Crown since 1603, and under the same Parliament since 1707, anyone who has travelled north of the border or even read a Scots newspaper can be in no doubt that the English and the Scots are still two very distinct nations. Naturally the Stuart monarchs of the seventeenth century, in particular James II and his daughter Queen Anne, retained a great affection for all things Scots but it was the Hanoverian Queen Victoria and her German husband Prince Albert who, well over a century later, rekindled the Royal Family's close personal links with Scotland. They bought Balmoral and modelled it as a holiday home where they could enjoy family life in the peace and privacy of the Scottish countryside which they both came to love so much. The present Queen Mother, who is a Scot herself, bought a Scottish castle, the Castle of May, as a retreat following the death of George VI. In spite of her continuing involvement in public life it remains her best loved home. Her daughter, Elizabeth II, has shown an affection for Balmoral that is nearly as great as that of Queen Victoria. Every year the Royal Family go to Scotland for the greater part of the summer to recharge their batteries and to take part in the local sport and festivities like the Braemar Gathering, which give them real enjoyment.

Yet the Queen's visits to Scotland are by no means all private holidays. The Queen is Queen of Scotland as well as of England and each year she has quite separate ceremonial duties to perform there.

THE HONOURS OF SCOTLAND

The Sovereign is crowned at Westminster Abbey on a Coronation Chair which contains the Stone of Scone. This is the Stone of Destiny which some Scots believed had been the pillow used by Jacob when he had his dream of the angels ascending into heaven. The ancient legend connected with this stone was that the monarch who sat on it would control the Scots and that equally the Scots would reign wherever the stone was taken. Contemptuous of the legend, the Hammer of the Scots, the English King Edward I, captured the Stone of Scone and took it back to England to be incorporated in the Coronation Chair at Westminster Abbey. Eventually, however, the prophecy came to fulfilment, though not in Edward's time, for in 1603 James I and VI came from Scotland to be crowned King of England on the chair containing the Scottish Coronation stone. So at last the Scots reigned in England and the English King reigned in Scotland.

The Stone of Scone has been part of the English Coronation ritual since it was captured in 1296 and many Scots would like to see it returned. However, the Scots still have their Regalia, known as the Honours of Scotland. These are kept on display in the Crown Room at Edinburgh Castle. The most important of the Scottish Crown Jewels, the Honours Three, are the Crown of Robert the Bruce, the Sword of State presented in 1507 to James IV by Pope Julius II, and the Sceptre.

The Crown is built up from a plain gold circlet worn by Robert the Bruce round his helmet. It is uncertain whether or not it is the one he wore at the battle of Bannockburn or whether it was made immediately afterwards as a memento of his great victory over the English. This circlet was embellished with diamonds, sapphires, pearls, and other rich jewels. In the sixteenth century James v had the Crown mended and augmented. The two imperial arches which were added are believed to have been fashioned in gold from the king's own Scottish gold mine.

The Sword of State is five feet long. It was presented to James iv by Pope Julius ii while Scotland was still a Catholic nation, as a reminder of his duty to be a Defender of the Faith. Although Scotland has had an official Calvinist church since the end of the sixteenth century the Sword of State still keeps its place of honour among the Regalia, being regarded now as a symbol of the Sovereign's determination to defend the liberties of the people.

The Sceptre is a traditional symbol of royal authority, not just in Scotland but in most European cultures. The early Scots invested their king with a white wand as a symbol of power. The present Sceptre, which is over three feet long, was reputedly another Papal gift. It was largely remodelled by James v and is decorated with carved figures of the Virgin Mary, St Andrew, the patron saint of Scotland, and St James.

Because of the chaos of the English civil war in the middle of the seventeenth century, when many Scots supported the Stuart cause, the Honours of Scotland were hidden away until the Restoration of 1660. When the Parliaments of England and Scotland were united in 1707 many Scots feared that the Crown Jewels would be taken away to England so they were concealed again. In 1818 they were rediscovered by a State Commission urged on to a great extent by Sir Walter Scott who had an incurably romantic love of all things Scottish and of Scottish royalty in particular.

The remainder of the Stuart jewels which had been taken out of the country were left to the English Crown by Henry, Duke of York. He was a Roman Catholic Cardinal and brother of the last direct Stuart claimant to the throne, Prince Charles Edward Stuart. The bequest was in recognition of George iii's kindness in settling a pension on him after he had been left destitute by the French Revolution in 1789. In 1830 George iii's son, William iv, directed that the Jewels be returned to Scotland to be kept in the Crown Room with the Honours Three. These Stuart heirlooms include Charles i's ruby and diamond Coronation ring, the St Andrew, a figure of the patron saint of Scotland carved on an onyx, which opens to reveal a portrait of Anne of Denmark, wife of James i and vi, and the gold collar of the Order of the Garter, which Elizabeth i presented to her heir, the future James i and vi.

George iv, who eventually succeeded to the throne in 1821 after many

George IV in Highland dress

years as Regent for his incapacitated father, was anxious to effect a permanent reconciliation between the Stuarts and the Hanoverians. Consequently in 1822 he made his famous visit to Scotland – the first English king to make a State visit there since James II in 1688. It was stage managed by Sir Walter Scott to whom George while still Prince Regent had given the commission to uncover the Crown Jewels hidden away at Edinburgh Castle. The later Hanoverians' reconciliation with their Scottish subjects was greatly advanced by George IV's attitude. He loved the romantic side of Scottish history and had a genuine enthusiasm for

Scottish traditions and customs which he shared with his friend Sir Walter Scott. George IV's Coronation pageantry was greatly influenced by Scott's view of history, particularly his books *Ivanhoe* and *Kenilworth*. During the 1822 State visit George gave his official approval to Highland dress, which had been banned as a symbol of disloyalty from 1748, after the Jacobite uprisings, until 1792. He appeared at a levée at Holyroodhouse in full highland uniform including a kilt in Stuart tartan under which he wore flesh coloured pantaloons in order to preserve the decencies! At the Caledonian Hunt Ball he insisted 'No foreign dances. I dislike seeing anything in Scotland that is not purely national and characteristic.' It was George IV who granted the Royal Company of Archers the privilege of being the Sovereign's Bodyguard for Scotland (see p. 54).

Despite the undoubted warm feelings held by the Royal Family towards Scotland since that time there has been no revival of a separate Scottish coronation. Charles II, like his father and grandfather, went through a separate Scottish coronation, and he was the last monarch to do so. He was crowned at Scone on New Year's Day 1651, two years after his father Charles I was beheaded. That coronation confirmed his position as King of the Scots but he had to wait until 1660 to be crowned King of England as well. When George IV visited Edinburgh after his English coronation he did not go through a separate Scottish coronation, but the Crown Jewels were brought out of the Crown House and put on display.

In 1953 Elizabeth II paid a State visit to Scotland after her own Coronation in Westminster Abbey. In the spirit which has led to the revival of much ceremonial in this reign it was decided to hold a Royal Progress from Holyroodhouse to St Giles's Cathedral. For this the Honours were brought out and borne before the Queen. The Sceptre and Sword travelled in one coach (the Sword carried by the Earl of Home who later, as Sir Alec Douglas-Home, became Prime Minister) and the Crown followed in another. By the side of each coach, as well as next to the Queen's coach, marched an escort of Royal Archers of the Queen's Bodyguard for Scotland. It remains to be seen whether or not Prince Charles will eventually follow his namesakes and hold a totally separate Scottish coronation though it might well prove a popular decision in Scotland.

HOLYROODHOUSE

Edinburgh was originally named Edwinesburgh after its founder King Edwin of Northumbria. In 1437 James II of Scotland decided to make it the Scottish capital instead of Perth. Holy Rood or Holyroodhouse as it was renamed in 1931, became the favoured residence of the Scottish monarchs. However, when George IV paid his State visit to Scotland he chose to stay not at Holyroodhouse but at Dalkeith Palace, the home of the

Holyroodhouse, the Queen's official Edinburgh residence

Scotts of Buccleuch. Queen Victoria, on her many visits to Scotland, stayed occasionally at Holyroodhouse, using it as a stopping off point on her journey to Balmoral. The present century has seen the Palace restored to its former importance as the official residence of the Sovereign in Scotland, although Balmoral remains the private residence.

Holyroodhouse is at the opposite end of the Royal Mile from Edinburgh Castle. It was originally built as the guest house of Holy Rood Abbey. The Abbey entertained many visitors because it housed a famous relic believed to be a fragment of Christ's cross (rood) which many pilgrims came to see. Several Scottish kings were buried in the church there including James v, the father of Mary Queen of Scots. Darnley, the husband whose murder she is thought to have plotted with Bothwell, is also buried there. A large part of the Palace was burnt down by the English in 1543. In 1671 Charles II undertook a major restoration of the entire Palace, styling it on the lines of a French château both as a tribute to the 'Auld Alliance' which had existed for centuries between the French and the Scots, and because of his own admiration for all things French. During the 1745 campaign the young Pretender, Prince Charles Edward Stuart, held a ball at the Palace.

Holyroodhouse is the scene of most of the Queen's official duties in Scotland. Investitures are held at the Palace and so are Garden Parties. The residence is also used when State visits are made when the Queen is staying in Scotland. On these and other State occasions the Queen usually travels in the Scottish State Coach, which has been adapted from a coach built in 1830 by the addition of glass panels which make the Queen and her visitors more visible to the crowd.

If the Queen arrives in Edinburgh, in her official capacity, to stay at Holyroodhouse, one small ceremony which always takes place is the Presentation of the Keys of the City, These Keys, which were first made for an official visit by Charles I in 1646, are taken from a red velvet cushion carried by the City Chamberlain and presented to Her Majesty by the Lord Provost. Similarly when the Queen arrives at her Palace she is officially handed the Keys by the Hereditary Keeper of the Palace of Holyroodhouse, an appointment made by Charles I during the same visit. The Hereditary Keeper is always the Duke of Hamilton. He, in his turn, appoints a Bailie who controls the Holyrood Constables. Although theoretically the Constables ensure the security of the Palace their function is now almost entirely ceremonial. From them a Guard of Honour is selected to be on duty at occasions such as the Holyroodhouse Garden Parties. They wear a distinctive blue uniform with a cockaded silk hat approved by George V in 1914.

EDINBURGH CASTLE

Before the Scottish kings took over the more comfortable quarters of the guest house of Holy Rood Abbey they lived in the Castle at the other end of the Royal Mile. The Scots kings had great need of a fortified residence for few of them died natural deaths: those who were not killed in battle were generally murdered by others anxious to replace them. There was a fortress on the site in the Bronze Age but its recorded history goes back to the eleventh century when it was the home of Malcolm III and his English wife, Margaret, who was canonized after her death because of her good works. The chapel she built in 1076 is the only part of the Castle which survives from that date and it is named St Margaret's Chapel in her honour. Robert the Bruce had much of the Castle destroyed in 1313 to prevent its being used by the English and it was rebuilt in the middle of the fourteenth century.

The history associated with the Castle is rich and varied. The Great Hall, built in 1483, housed the first Scottish Parliaments. Mary Queen of Scots' son, who was later to unite England and Scotland as James I and VI when Elizabeth I produced no heir, was born at Edinburgh Castle in 1566. Both Charles I and Charles II stayed there prior to their Scottish coronations. When the Scots Heralds proclaimed Charles II King at the Mercat Cross Oliver Cromwell exacted his revenge by taking over the Castle.

Royal Salutes are fired from the battlements of Edinburgh Castle as they are at Hyde Park and the Tower in London. The famous cannon Mons Meg, which was cast by the master gunner of James IV, Mary Queen of Scots' grandfather, can still be seen although it was put out of action by a particularly vigorous salute it fired for Charles II in 1680.

When a new General Officer Commanding Scotland is appointed he becomes Governor of the Castle. This happens every three years and necessitates a ceremony of Installation. This is yet another piece of ritual which was re-established in this century. It was revived in 1936 after a lapse of nearly eighty years. The ceremony takes place on the Castle Esplanade. The new Governor arrives at the Gate of the Castle, accompanied by the Lord Lyon King of Arms, the heralds, and Scottish State Trumpeters. The Gate is shut. When the Trumpeters sound a fanfare the alarm is sounded in the Castle and the Castle Garrison Commander, sword drawn, appears on the ramparts with his Adjutant. Lord Lyon approaches and is challenged.

'Halt. Who comes there?'

'The Lord Lyon King of Arms'.

'What comes the Lord Lyon King of Arms to do at the gates of Edinburgh Castle?'

The Lord Lyon explains he has come in the name of the Queen to command the gates to be opened to the new Governor.

Not easily deceived, the Garrison Commander asks to see a copy ('just double') of the orders. A herald takes this to the gate and when he has knocked three times the small door in the gate is opened and the document taken from him. When the Garrison Commander is sure there is no trickery afoot he gives the command for the gate to be opened. The Key of the Castle is brought under escort to the new Governor who touches it in a token gesture of acceptance and is himself accepted as bona fide. This interesting ceremony, which like the Ceremony of the Keys at the Tower of London dates back over 800 years, takes place every three years. Those wishing to watch should look for details in the Press. The present Governor was appointed in 1982.

LORD LYON AND THE HERALDS

The heralds in Scotland, like the heralds in England, are responsible for the organization of ceremonial and for the regulation and control of heraldic devices and coats of arms. Heraldry in Scotland differs from that of

England in several respects, most obviously in that it includes the clan tartans. The differences in the heraldry reflect the difference in the social structure of medieval England and Scotland, for Scotland was based largely round the family clans, a system totally unlike the English way of life. The Scottish heralds consist of the Lord Lyon King of Arms, the Rothesay, Marchmont and Albany Heralds, and the Unicorn, Ormond, and Carrick Pursuivants. As in England Extra-Ordinary Heralds may be appointed for particular occasions. Unlike the English heralds the Scottish heralds became part of the Civil Service in the last century.

The chief herald is the Lord Lyon King of Arms. He holds a very special position which combines the responsibility for State ceremonial which the Earl Marshal carries in England, together with the duties as chief herald and an officer of the Order of the Thistle which are similar to those carried out by his counterpart, Garter King of Arms, in England. Being the Senior Herald he, like Garter King of Arms, reads out the important Proclamations. This was once a major part of a herald's duties before the age of mass literacy. Like the Earl Marshal in England, Lord Lyon presides over the Court which has jurisdiction over all disputes to do with heraldry and genealogy. This Lyon Court has far greater powers than the Court of Claims in England and sits far more regularly, perhaps because there are so many people of Scots descent throughout the world who wish to re-establish contact with their families. Lord Lyon himself can trace his office back to the Courts of the Picts and the Scots. The office of Lord Lyon is generally thought to have evolved from that of the Druidic 'shennachy' whose job it was to relate the ancestry of the Scottish kings before their coronations at Scone. The shennachy kept all such important genealogical information in his head and passed it on by word of mouth before written records were kept.

Although he has no official capacity at a Westminster coronation the Lord Lyon is invited as a courtesy and as a reminder of the days when the shennachy performed the essential recitation of the royal pedigree.

Scottish heralds, including Lord Lyon, wear tabards similar to those of the English heralds. The royal arms with which they are embroidered are those which the Queen uses in Scotland. Ceremonies in which Lord Lyon and the heralds take place are:

Proclamations, including those of the Accession and Coronation. These take place from the balcony of the Mercat Cross, by the west door of St Giles's Cathedral, and occasionally from the gate of Edinburgh Castle and at Holyroodhouse.

The Thistle Service and Procession. This takes place annually at St Giles's Cathedral.

The Procession of the General Assembly of the Church of Scotland, which takes place in May.

The Installation of the new Governor at Edinburgh Castle. This takes place every three years on the Esplanade in front of the Castle.

The heralds also form part of the Procession which takes place in Edinburgh after the Accession of a new monarch, and Lord Lyon can be seen presiding over the Lyon Court, which has no fixed dates, and at the Head Courts of the Lord Lyon which are held at the beginning of May and near Halloween. These two dates correspond to 'Beltane' and 'Samhain' in the Druidic calendar, a reminder of the Lord Lyon's origins.

THE GENERAL ASSEMBLY

Scotland ceased to have its own Parliament after the Act of Union of 1707. The General Assembly of the Church of Scotland therefore became the nearest thing to a national assembly, and this impression was reinforced by the Church of Scotland's continual involvement with politics. This involvement was due to its determination to maintain the Protestant Scottish way of life, which it so firmly upheld, free from foreign, and particularly Catholic, interference.

The importance of the General Assembly in Scottish national life is indicated by the fact that during the week in which it is held the Queen appoints a Lord High Commissioner to act as Sovereign's representative for this one event only. To emphasize the Lord High Commissioner's role as representative of the Crown he or she lives throughout the week at Holyroodhouse and takes precedence over everyone else except the Queen and Duke of Edinburgh. Like the Queen the Lord High Commissioner is presented with the Keys of the City of Edinburgh on arriving to take up residence in Holyroodhouse, and is also given a 21-gun Royal Salute.

The Procession into the General Assembly is one of Scotland's major annual ceremonies. Leading the Procession are the heralds and pursuivants in their colourfully embroidered tabards. Behind them come the Hereditary Bearer of the St Andrew's Flag (the Earl of Lauderdale) and the Hereditary Bearer of the Royal Banner of Scotland (the Earl of Dundee). The Lord Lyon King of Arms comes at the end of this group. Next comes the Purse Bearer who precedes the Sovereign on the rare occasions when he or she is present in person. In 1960 the Queen was present for the 400th anniversary of its first meeting and in 1977 as part of her Silver Jubilee celebrations, but usually the Lord High Commissioner takes her place. Also in attendance are the Earl of Erroll and the Duke of Argyll in their capacity as Hereditary Lord High Constable and Hereditary Master of the Household in Scotland.

Once in the Assembly Hall the Sovereign or Sovereign's representative and the rest of the royal party sit in the Throne Gallery which runs across the back of the Hall. The Sovereign or Lord High Commissioner makes a speech from the throne but otherwise takes no part in the proceedings. Spiritual matters are considered no part of the Crown's province in Scotland.

Date **May for one week, see the Press.**
Time **See the Press.**
Place **Edinburgh, the Assembly Hall. The Procession into the Assembly Hall is sometimes preceded by a service in St Giles's Cathedral. For this there is a military guard of honour and a military band in Parliament Square. For details of this and other Scottish ceremonial see the Press or contact the Scottish Tourist Authority (see p. 176).**

Royal Weddings

Of all the 'occasional' royal ceremonies weddings best sum up the feelings evoked by the Royal Family and its traditions. It is often said that the Royal Family by its separateness and the ritual which surrounds its celebrations does not alienate itself from the people but rather, because it reflects in a larger than life fashion the day-to-day occurrences of the unknown families in the country, adds its own special mystique to the lives of each and every one of us. The importance of the family and its milestones is shored up by the seriousness with which the Royal Family of today takes family life. This attitude was begun and fostered by Queen Victoria and Prince Albert. The constitutional historian, Walter Bagehot, writing in the nineteenth century was well aware of this aspect of the monarch's role. 'A princely marriage is the brilliant edition of a universal fact, and as such it rivets mankind.' Today mankind is more riveted than ever for the royal weddings, which were once private occasions, have become public spectacles which rival the Coronation in the interest and emotion they provoke. When permission was refused in 1923 for the wedding of the Duke of York, later George VI, and Elizabeth Bowes-Lyon to be broadcast on the radio, no one could have anticipated that the wedding of their grandson would attract a world-wide television audience estimated at 500 million.

The earliest royal marriages, indeed most of those up to the time of Queen Victoria herself, had either a partially or a totally political motive. This could sometimes lead to personality clashes of major proportions. Henry II and Eleanor of Aquitaine, both extremely strong characters, eventually clashed so irrevocably that Eleanor was imprisoned by her husband for the ten years up until his death in 1189. But not all arranged marriages were empty shells. When Henry VII married Elizabeth of York, the niece of Richard III whom he had just usurped, his aim was simply to unite the warring factions of Lancaster and York for good. However, there is every indication that the marriage was a happy one, and there are touching accounts of her attempts to console him after the death of their eldest son Prince Arthur in 1502.

Earlier in history the death of Richard II's queen, Anne of Bohemia, in 1394, left him so distraught that he had the wing of the palace at Sheen, where she had died, burnt down. The Earl of Arundel, who appeared late for her funeral at Westminster Abbey, was knocked to the ground by the King and sent to the Tower for a week. When Eleanor of Castile died in 1290 after thirty-six years of happy marriage to Edward I he erected a stone cross at each of the places where her body rested overnight on its journey from Harby, near Lincoln, to Westminster Abbey. The last and best-known of these, Charing Cross, like all but three of the twelve original crosses, has disappeared, but a replica was built in 1863.

Political marriages were not infrequently the beginning of successful personal relationships. But sometimes when marriage was a matter of politics rather than personal preference, like arranging chess-pieces on a board, the arrangements did not fall easily into place. Lord Hervey recalls the irascible George II's dilemma over a wife for his heir, Frederick. 'For Protestant princesses there is not a great choice of matches. The Princess of Denmark he would not have. The Princesses of Prussia had a madman for their father, and I did not think ingrafting my half-witted coxcomb upon a madwoman would mend the breed.' George II's great grandson, the Prince Regent, knowing that it was his political duty to marry and provide an heir, needed a vast quantity of drink to get him to the altar with Caroline of Brunswick – 'he looked like death, and full of confusion, as if he wished to hide himself from the looks of the whole world'. Despite the dynastic reasons for their marriage, Caroline and George separated for good after the birth of their only child, Princess Charlotte. Their incompatibility brought them to the divorce court, despite the political reasons for the union.

So even in the days of arranged marriages royal marriages were seen to be no different in essence from the marriages, successful or unsuccessful, of the king's subjects.

Now that political alliance is not expected to play a part in the pro-

The wedding of Prince Charles and Lady Diana Spencer in July 1981 had a world-wide audience of about 500 million, and crowds of well-wishers filled London

ceedings a wedding is an even better opportunity for the public to feel the similarity in all but outward show between their lives and those of the Royal Family. This change in emphasis was largely due to Queen Victoria. Her son, Edward, Prince of Wales, was encouraged to marry the beautiful Danish Princess Alexandra, less because a dynastic alliance was called for than because she was of suitable rank and age. (Indeed pro-Prussian Victoria had her misgivings 'The beauty of Denmark is much against our wishes. What a pity she is who she is.') Edward, unlike many of his ancestors, was at least allowed a chance to glimpse his bride-to-be in Cologne Cathedral before committing himself finally to the match.

A family wedding in the Chapel Royal when the Princess Royal (daughter of Queen Victoria) married Prince Frederick William of Prussia in 1858

By the time Princess Louise came to be married Queen Victoria had definite views on the desirability of foreign alliances. Princess Louise wished to marry the Marquess of Lorne, later the Duke of Argyll. Far from being put out Queen Victoria wrote to the Prince of Wales, 'Times have changed, great foreign alliances are looked on as causes of trouble and anxiety and are of no good. What could be more painful than the position in which our family were placed during the wars with Denmark, and between Prussia and Austria? Every family feeling was rent asunder and we were powerless.' Since then, while many of Victoria's descendants have married into the royal families of Europe and become kings and queens by doing so, political considerations have been almost non-existent. There is no longer even a pretence that a royal marriage could have any bearing on foreign policy.

Royal marriages do still differ from those of ordinary people in some respects because they are subject to the Act of Settlement, 1701. As a result of this Act any member of the family who marries a Catholic forfeits his or her place in the succession. Also by the terms of the Royal Marriages Act of 1772 descendents of George III, other than those of princesses who have married into foreign royal houses, have to seek and obtain the consent of the Sovereign to their marriages which can be withheld if they are under twenty-five. This Act was a direct result of George III's concern for the unsuitable liaisons being made by his rather licentious brothers, several of whom, like his sons, including the Prince Regent, went through a form of marriage with a woman who would be considered unsuitable not just by their father but by the country as a whole. In addition marriage to a divorced person is still a problem, since the Sovereign is Head of the Anglican Church which does not officially approve of divorce or the re-marriage of divorced people in church – as Prince Michael of Kent discovered when he wished to marry the Catholic divorcée Baroness Marie-Christine von Reibnitz. Although the Queen willingly gave her consent the fact that the Baroness was a Catholic meant that the Prince had to renounce his place in the Line of Succession. However, since he wished his children to be restored to the Line of Succession the decision was made that any children should be brought up as Anglicans. As a result the Pope, who had granted the divorced Baroness an annulment of her previous marriage, refused to allow them to be married in a Catholic church. This gave rise to the unforeseen complication that they could not therefore marry in England at all, because since the Baroness was divorced she could not marry in an Anglican church. Because of the Pope's ruling they could not marry in a Catholic church in England. Because it had never been envisaged that a member of the Royal Family would wish to marry in a Register Office there was no provision made for such an eventuality in the Marriages Act of 1949. The problem was solved by a civil ceremony in the Baroness's native Vienna followed by a church blessing. The marriage of Prince Michael emphasized that although royal marriages are now fundamentally private concerns they are still hampered by out-dated conventions which on the whole do not trouble other people.

The marriages of Princess Margaret, Princess Alexandra, and Princess Anne, all three of whom married commoners, underlined the comparative informality of royal marriage today. Although Antony Armstrong-Jones became Earl of Snowdon immediately prior to his marriage, Angus Ogilvy and Mark Phillips declined any title. As a result Princess Alexandra and Princess Anne in addition to the style and title Her Royal Highness also chose to carry the more prosaic title of Mrs, Princess Alexandra becoming the Hon. Mrs Angus Ogilvy and Princess Anne – Mrs Mark Phillips. This move towards readily accepting a title lower in the social scale had really started with Princess Patricia of Connaught. Known as Patsy to her friends, the Princess was a grand-daughter of Queen Victoria. Her father was Arthur Duke of Connaught. Always modern in outlook the Princess

Crowds lined the streets to see Princess Patricia, youngest daughter of the Duke of Connaught, and her bridegroom, the Hon. Alexander Ramsay, in 1919

did not marry until she was thirty-two, when in 1919 she married Commander the Hon. Alexander Ramsay. Perhaps it was her response to the new mood in Europe after the terrible experience of the First World War, but the Princess startled everyone by announcing that on her marriage she intended to relinquish the style and title of Royal Highness and be known as (comparatively) plain Lady Patricia Ramsay. Even Princess Alexandra and Princess Anne, while embracing the title of Mrs, did not go so far as to drop the status of Royal Highness. Princess Patricia of Connaught not only set the tone for later royal weddings by relinquishing her title, but also began another tradition, that of holding royal weddings in Westminster Abbey. People were surprised in 1981 that Prince Charles and Lady Diana Spencer chose to marry in St Paul's Cathedral for in the sixty years since Princess Patricia's marriage the Abbey has been the setting for all royal weddings of importance. Its 'rightness' is partly because it is on a scale appropriate to the publicity which increasingly surrounds such events. It also seems particularly appropriate because it is the setting for all the coronations. Not surprisingly many people felt that Prince Charles had dispensed with a long established tradition by not marrying there, but in fact the 'tradition' does not even go back as far as the First World War.

Indeed before the mass media made royal weddings such public events, it was far more customary to celebrate them in private chapels with only a small number of guests. The flamboyant Charles II married Catherine of Braganza in Portsmouth with very little ceremony. Charles's niece, the future Queen Mary, married Prince William of Orange, later to be joint Sovereign with her, before an altar temporarily put up in her bedroom.

Queen Victoria's parents, the Duke of Kent and Dowager Princess of Saxe-Meiningen, were married at Dowager Queen Charlotte's home, the Dutch House at Kew, in a double wedding with the future William IV and Princess Adelaide of Saxe-Meiningen.

By the time Victoria herself married in 1840 at the Chapel Royal at St James's Palace, things were already beginning to change. There were 300 guests at the wedding, many of them political invitations, and the wedding itself was reported in the newspapers in some detail. As they set off for their honeymoon at Windsor they were accompanied by cheering crowds running beside their carriage. When twenty-three years later Victoria's son, the Prince of Wales, married Princess Alexandra of Denmark in St George's Chapel, Windsor, the Queen's deliberate avoidance of publicity (which she felt was not in keeping with the mourning for the recent death of Prince Albert) caused real offence. By this date the public had come to expect a wedding with publicity and pageantry almost as a matter of right. One journalist wrote rather grumpily, that if they had been so anxious to avoid publicity why had they not simply made a bare announcement in *The Times* along the lines 'On 10 March 1863, at St George's Chapel Windsor, Edward England to Alexandra Denmark'.

However, when Edward and Alexandra's son, the Duke of York, later George V, married Princess Mary of Teck in 1893, the sense of holiday and public participation were totally restored. The gossip columnist of *The Sketch* gave a lively description of the public nature of the wedding.

I mixed on wedding-day with the unwashed in St James's Park. Heavens! how unsavoury is hot humanity. The sun poured down, the people steamed up, while smiles and good humour reigned over all. I clung to the railings before the palace, kept a handkerchief offering incense to my nose, and for reward saw everything. . . . Extra merriment was caused when a seedy man, under the influence of ginger beer and sun probably, sat down in the middle of the cleared roadway, and declined to move until four policemen united their persuasions. For comicality and stolid good nature commend me to an English mob.'

Thirty years later when the Duke of York married Lady Elizabeth Bowes-Lyon there was an even greater sense of public holiday as 6,000 people waited to see the bride leave her home for Westminster Abbey. In 1947 there were 3,000 guests at the wedding of Princes Elizabeth to the Duke of Edinburgh, ten times as many as were at the wedding of Queen Victoria. While 300 million people watched the wedding of Princess Margaret which was televised from the Abbey in 1960. In 1981 nearly twice that many people were watching. Clearly although they are not truly State occasions, royal weddings in this day and age have become almost our most popular royal ceremonial events.

Like all ceremonies the weddings usually follow a set pattern, with additional individual interest being added by the details of the bride's dress, engagement ring, and choice of honeymoon location. One custom which makes royal weddings a little different is that it is usual for the Sovereign to foot the bill, whether it is a male or female child who is marrying. Other items such as extra policing are paid for by the State. Because it is a 'family occasion' a wedding, like a funeral, is master-minded by the Lord Chamberlain. (For important State occasions like the Coronation overall control is in the hands of the hereditary Earl Marshal of England, the Duke of Norfolk.) On behalf of the Sovereign the Lord Chamberlain issues the invitations and arranges the seating in the church. This takes into account the fact that the Royal Family always sits on the right hand side of the church so that the usual arrangement of guests, bridegroom's on the right, bride's on the left, may not apply. There may also be foreign and local dignitaries and politicians whose sense of priority and importance has to be catered for. Princess Anne chose not to have Heads of State at her wedding while King Juan Carlos did not come to Prince Charles's wedding, which was a family event for him, because he wished to make a political gesture as Head of the Spanish State.

The wedding pageantry begins with a procession from Buckingham Palace to the church, which is often, though not always, Westminster Abbey. If the bride is a member of the Royal Family she will travel in the 1910 glass coach, which was built for the Coronation of George v and re-furbished for the wedding of Princess Anne. Lady Diana Spencer also travelled to her wedding from Clarence House in the glass coach. Otherwise the bride will probably travel from her home in a landau, as Lady Elizabeth Bowes-Lyon did in 1923, or in one of the Queen's cars as Princess Alexandra did.

The processional route is lined with soldiers, including Guardsmen from the Household Division, and there is an Escort of Household Cavalry. Inside the church as well as at the entrance there may be members of the Sovereign's Bodyguard. Also on duty at the church are soldiers of regiments particularly associated with the member of the Royal Family who is getting married. For example when Princess Anne married Captain Mark Phillips, there were men from his regiment, the Queen's Dragoon Guards. It is customary for the wedding service to be performed by the Archbishop of Canterbury, although this is by no means a necessity. A minor tradition is that the bride's ring should be made from the nugget of Welsh gold which furnished the wedding rings of the Queen Mother, the Queen, Princess Margaret, Princess Anne, and the Princess of Wales. Similarly the wedding bouquet usually contains a piece of myrtle from a bush at Osborne, Isle of Wight, which was grown from the sprig in Queen Victoria's bouquet. At the end of the service the couple curtsey and bow to the Queen as they leave, a gesture of courtesy towards someone who, however much of a 'family' occasion it may be, can rarely be allowed to forget that she is also Head of Church and State.

The wedding is followed by a State drive back to Buckingham Palace. On their return the newly-married couple travel together in the glass coach which was designed to give the crowds a good view of the occupants. Because the wedding of the Prince of Wales in 1981 took place in the summer the crowds got an even better view than usual, as the royal couple took a gamble on the weather and travelled back to the Palace in the State landau.

Shortly after their arrival the couple, together with the rest of the Royal Family, make their appearance on the balcony to acknowledge the enthusiasm of the crowd. After this they go in for the wedding breakfast and the pageantry is at an end. The royal wedding becomes much the same as any other family's wedding, right down to the photographs taken for the family album, and, as in the case of the Prince of Wales's wedding, large blue and silver balloons tied to the back of the going-away carriage, with a 'Just Married' notice on the back which is a tradition by no means confined to the Royal Family.

The local and national Press will carry full details of the arrangements for a royal wedding, and there is always an official programme on sale in advance. The tourist authorities will also be able to supply full details.

Royal Funerals

The funeral of a monarch, or someone close to the throne, like Lord Mountbatten of Burma, can never be a truly private occasion for the family itself. Because of what the person represents he or she is mourned by the nation as well as by relatives and friends. The private preference of the family might be for something simpler and more personal but an elaborate funeral, complete with pomp and pageantry, is a way of channelling all the emotions evoked by the death into a ritual which in some way helps to wipe the slate clean and prepare people for the new order. The traditional means of announcing the death of the king sums it up so neatly, 'The King is Dead! Long Live the King!'

Royal funerals are only for Sovereigns. Others may be accorded a State funeral, which in the case of Winston Churchill or Earl Mountbatten

may seem almost more grand. Although State funerals may be as elaborate, if not more so, than royal funerals one of the differences between them is that a State funeral is paid for by the State and organized by the Earl Marshal of England, the Duke of Norfolk. Private royal funerals are the responsibility of the Great Officer of the Household, the Lord Chamberlain, who is also responsible for that happier, but equally personal, royal ceremony, the Royal Wedding. For the funeral of a Sovereign the Lord Chamberlain works in close conjunction with the Earl Marshal.

One of the reasons why the Sovereign's funeral may seem less magnificent than that of a distinguished subject like Winston Churchill is that the service takes place in St George's Chapel, Windsor. This has a much smaller capacity than St Paul's Cathedral or Westminster Abbey, which have been the setting for most full scale State funerals. Holding the actual funeral service and committal at Windsor gives the Royal Family a chance for relative privacy in their bereavement after the pageantry and ritual of the Lying-in-State and the Funeral Procession.

In 1547 Henry VIII chose to be buried at Windsor in order to lie next to the one wife who had given him a son, and died as a result, Jane Seymour. However it was not until over two centuries later that George III, who spent his declining years at Windsor, had a royal vault constructed under St George's Chapel. In the following century Queen Victoria, totally bereft after the death of Prince Albert, built a mausoleum for them both at Frogmore in the Home Park at Windsor. She intended it to be a memorial to their life together and she knew he would not have liked the gloomy vault shared with others. It is now customary for British Sovereigns and members of the Royal Family to be buried at Windsor either in St George's itself or in the royal burial ground at Frogmore.

Consternation was caused in 1843 by the inexplicable wish of the dying Duke of Sussex, an uncle of Queen Victoria, to be buried at Kensal Green cemetery. Greville, the contemporary diarist, writes in his memoirs:

He placed the Court in great embarrassment by leaving directions that he should be buried at the cemetery in the Harrow Road; and there was a grand consultation yesterday, whether this arrangement should be carried into effect, or whether the queen should take on herself to have him buried with the rest of the Royal Family at Windsor . . . the discussion about the Duke of Sussex's funeral ended by his being buried with Royal honours at Kensal Green. It all went off very decently and in an orderly manner.

Before Windsor became the accepted place for royal burials most British Sovereigns were interred at Westminster Abbey. Although the Abbey made a splendid setting for the service and ceremony its very size and accessibility to the crowds and to London society sometimes contributed to the occasion being more of a shambles than it should have been.

Lord Mountbatten was accorded a State Funeral after his assassination, 1979

145

George III's decision to construct a family vault at Windsor may have been influenced by the chaos he witnessed at the funeral of his grandfather, George II. Horace Walpole described the scene in a letter to a friend. First there was the impressive and solemn ritual:

I had never seen a royal funeral. . . . It is absolutely a noble sight. The Prince's chamber hung with purple, and a quantity of silver lamps, the coffin under a canopy of purple velvet, and six vast chandeliers of silver on high stands, had a very good effect. . . . The procession through a line of foot guards, every seventh man bearing a torch, the horse guards lining the outside their officers with drawn sabres and crape sashes on horseback, the drums muffled, the fifes, bells tolling, and minute guns, – all this was very solemn. But the charm was the entrance of the Abbey, where we were received by the Dean and Chapter in rich robes, the choir and alms-men bearing torches; the whole Abbey so illuminated, that one saw it to greater advantage than by day.

Unfortunately things went downhill from that moment, in sharp contrast to the meticulous organization of such events today by the Earl Marshal and the Lord Chamberlain.

When we came to the chapel of Henry the Seventh all solemnity and decorum ceased; no order was observed, people sat or stood where they could or would; the yeomen of the guard were crying out for help, oppressed by the immense weight of the coffin; the Bishop read sadly and blundered in the prayers; and the anthem, besides being immeasurably tedious, would have served as well for a nuptial.

In 1837 Greville was to record similar sentiments in his description of the funeral of William IV.

A soldier's funeral . . . was more impressive, more decent, more affecting than all this pomp with pasteboard crowns, and heralds scampering about, while idleness and indifference were gazing or gossiping about the royal remains. . . . The service was intolerably long and tedious, and miserably read by the Dean of Windsor.

The reference to the heralds is a reminder that for hundreds of years they had played an important part in organizing the funerals, not just of the Sovereign and Royal Family, but of many of those whose position entitled them to bear arms. As already mentioned the heralds had started out as tournament organizers and had progressed to being the arbiters of all matters to do with genealogy and coats of arms (see p. 96). Their involvement in the organization of funerals and the correct ordering of all the varied accoutrements was a logical development. Funerals had different degrees of pageantry and paraphernalia depending on the rank of the person being buried. The arranging and providing of these various requirements was a lucrative business and the heralds guarded their monopoly fiercely. They were also paid for taking death certificates which recorded significant details about the life and issue of the deceased. A heraldic funeral certificate was taken for the funeral of Sir Winston Churchill in 1965, but even by the eighteenth century the custom was already in decline.

The funeral of Queen Elizabeth I is described in detail by Henry Chattle, a contemporary. From it we know that Elizabeth's funeral was very much a heraldic funeral. The cortège was led by the pursuivants and the hereditary standard bearers carrying emblems such as the portcullis and the Lion and the Dragon which are heraldic symbols of the Crown. Dozens of banners were carried including the great banner of England escorted by the heralds. Garter King of Arms and Clarenceux Herald followed behind the riderless royal horse. Even today it is customary for the deceased's horse to be led in the procession as it was at the funeral of Earl Mountbatten. One element of Elizabeth's funeral which was customary for royal funerals at the time but which has long since been omitted was the effigy of the Queen which lay on top of the hearse, 'the lively picture of her Majesty's whole body in her parliament robes, with a crown on her head and a sceptre in her hands, lying on top of the corpse enshrined in lead and enbalmed'. Another contemporary, Stow, wrote that the sight of it provoked 'such a general sighing, groaning and weeping as the like hath not been seen or known in the memory of man'.

Now that the Sovereign is buried in the comparative privacy of Windsor the State pageantry centres round the Lying-in-State and the Funeral Procession.

Three of the last four monarchs have lain in state in Westminster Hall. This is the only part of the original Palace of Westminster which survived the great fire which destroyed the rest. This historic building is a fitting setting for such a solemn occasion. Since it was built by William II in 1097 it has been closely associated with the history of the Royal Family and the country. Here Edward II was forced to abdicate in 1327 and Richard II was deposed in 1399. Charles I was condemned to death by Parliament in Westminster Hall in 1649. From Stephen to George IV a sumptuous Coronation Banquet was held in the Hall after every coronation. A plaque on the wall marks the historic occasion when Charles I forced his way from Westminster Hall to St Stephen's Hall where the House of Commons was sitting and by his demands for the arrest of five of the Members sparked off the English Civil War.

The royal coffin is received at Westminster Hall by the Archbishop of Canterbury together with the two men involved in the funeral arrangements, the Earl Marshal and the Lord Chamberlain. Also present are the heralds and Black Rod. The coffin is placed on a catafalque in the centre of the Hall. On top of it are placed the symbols of royalty, including the Crown. They are a reminder of the time when the monarch's effigy wearing

147

Keeping vigil in Sandringham Church by the coffin of George VI are the head keeper and three other keepers from Sandringham (1952)

George V Lying-in-State in Westminster Hall, 1936

the insignia was placed on the coffin. Three groups of soldiers have the privilege of keeping vigil over the catafalque. They are men of the two Royal Bodyguards, the Honourable Corps of Gentlemen at Arms, and the Queen's Bodyguard of the Yeomen of the Guard, and the Regiments of the Household Division. They stand with their arms reversed and with their heads bowed as the public file in to pay homage to the late Sovereign. At about midnight before the funeral of George V his four sons, including the new King Edward VIII, in full dress uniform, took their places by the catafalque and kept their own vigil while the last of the public shuffled past.

After the tranquility of the Lying-in-State comes the pageantry of the Funeral Procession. Hundreds of years ago this would have gone direct to Westminster Abbey as Queen Elizabeth's procession did. Now it goes from Westminster Hall to Paddington Station where it is put on the train to Windsor. The entire route is lined with troops all, like those keeping vigil at the catafalque, with their arms reversed. Throughout the Procession solemn music is played by military bands. Almost inevitably whenever old film of Queen Victoria's funeral procession is shown it is accompanied by Handel's gloomy 'Funeral March'. This is misleading for Victoria, despite her interest in death, disliked funerals which were unnecessarily black and depressing. She had specified her own music, which included Highland laments and works by Chopin and Beethoven.

The coffin is carried on a gun carriage which is provided by the Royal Horse Artillery. They used also to provide the horses to pull it, but during Queen Victoria's Funeral Procession a mishap occurred which gave rise to what is now an important feature of the ritual surrounding a Sovereign's funeral. The Procession from Waterloo Station to Paddington (Queen Victoria had lain in state at Osborne and her body was brought by ship and train to London) had gone as planned. Unfortunately when the body

arrived at Windsor station one of the horses which had been waiting there ready to pull the gun carriage up the hill to the Castle became temporarily out of control and when it shied up it snapped the traces. The old Queen had expressly referred to the Procession in her will, emphasizing that it 'ought to be properly arranged', yet for a short while it looked as if it would have to be cut short and the gun carriage moved up to the Castle by the quickest possible route. However, Prince Louis of Battenburg quickly arranged that the Guard of Honour, which was made up of naval ratings, should pull the gun carriage along the processional route. This sight was so impressive that since then horses have been dispensed with. Naval ratings, over a hundred of them, pull the gun carriage bearing the coffin along the processional route both in London and Windsor. Winston Churchill was accorded the same honour because he had once been head of the Admiralty.

The burial service at St George's Chapel is semi-private, but even so there is a certain amount of ceremonial which is unique to the funeral of a Sovereign. The Bearer Party is always made up from men of the King's or Queen's Company of the Grenadier Guards, which is the senior Guards regiment. Men from this company always escort the coffin during the Funeral Procession as well.

The heralds are present at the service just as they were at the funeral service of Elizabeth I. Garter King of Arms proclaims the style and titles of the late Sovereign as has been done at royal funerals since the early Middle Ages.

The Camp Colour of the King's or Queen's Company of the Grenadier Guards is handed to the new Sovereign by the Lieutenant Commanding the regiment. This is placed on the coffin and buried with it. The new Sovereign presents the company with a new colour soon after.

Last of all the Lord Chamberlain breaks his wand of office over his knee. As already mentioned the wand is a symbol of royal power and is seen at its most magnificent form in the Sceptre carried by the Sovereign at the Coronation. Carrying a wand indicates that the bearer has been delegated to exercise a part of that power on behalf of the monarch. Breaking the wand signifies that that power is no longer valid because the person from whom it derived is now dead. All royal power from that moment comes from the new monarch, who may or may not wish to invest it in the same individuals. In past centuries not only the Lord Great Chamberlain but other Great Officers of State, the Lord Treasurer, Lord Steward, and Earl Marshal, did the same thing.

So the pageantry of a royal funeral is not just show but has deep significance as well. Its symbolism leaves no doubt that however sad the event the life of the nation, as personified by its Head of State, goes on without a break.

Full details of a royal funeral will be available in the local and national Press and from tourist authorities.

State Visits and Banquets

An integral part of the Sovereign's role, and one which usually involves a great deal of ceremonial, is to entertain other countries' Heads of State when they visit Britain.

The Queens entertains people on State visits an average of two or three times a year. Each visit requires at least three months of detailed planning and much of the day to day work is handled by the Comptroller of the Lord Chamberlain's office. Inevitably there are detailed schedules to arrange and there are the added complications of matters of protocol. By and large the arrangements for a State visit run smoothly along a well-established path but the routine is flexible enough to accommodate any potential difficulties.

Invitations are issued after consultation between the Foreign Office, Cabinet Office, and the Queen's Household. An invitation is never formally extended until it is already known that it will be accepted. The Queen may receive people for private visits who might not be acceptable to the Foreign Office if they came representing their country but a State visit is an act of diplomacy.

Official visits, although they were not called State visits until the last century, have taken place for many hundred of years. They give countries a chance unashamedly to impress one another with their organization and the entertainment they offer. The son of the Holy Roman Emperor was forced into such a visit when he was shipwrecked off the English coast in 1506. Henry VIII took advantage of the opportunity to entertain lavishly the son of a man he was extremely anxious to impress. William Makefyrr in a letter describing their meeting wrote, 'The King's Grace and the King of Castile met this day at three of the clock, upon Cleworth Green, two miles out of Windsor, and there the King received him in the goodliest manner that ever I saw, and each of them embraced the other in arms.' Having greeted each other they went on to Windsor 'and so went to the King of Castile's chamber, which is the richliest hanged that ever I saw; seven chambers together hanged with cloth of Arras wrought with gold as thick as could be; and as for three beds of estate, no king christened can shew such three.'

But as well as giving the country a chance to impress with the warmth and lavishness of the hospitality State visits offer a genuine chance to put international relations on a more relaxed and personal footing. For many centuries the Sovereigns who welcomed and gave hospitality to one another were related and their family relationships were one of the fundamental methods of conducting foreign policy. When Frederick, the Elector Palatine, arrived for a State visit in 1613 it was with the intention of marrying James I's daughter, the Princes Elizabeth. A contemporary, John Fynnet, witnessed his arrival:

The Count Palatine landed at Gravesend on Friday night last. . . . His Approach, Gesture and Countenance, were seasoned with a well-becoming confidence; and bending himself with a due Reverence before the King, he told him among other compliments, that in his Sight and Presence he enjoyed a great part (reserving it should seem the greatest to his Mistress) of the End and Happiness of his Journey. After turning to the Queen she entertained him with a fixed Countenance.

However the Queen overcame her initial dislike and the Princess was allowed to marry the Elector Palatine. Their descendants were the Hanoverian kings of England.

During Queen Victoria's reign royal marriages were no longer expected to form the essence of foreign policy, but the importance of State visits for cementing international friendships was well understood by the Queen herself. In a memorandum following the State visit to England of the Emperor Napoleon III of France in 1855, she wrote: 'with his particular character and views, which are very personal, a kind, unaffected and hearty reception by *us personally* in our own family will make a lasting impression on his mind; he will see that he can rely upon our friendship and honesty towards him and his country so long as he remains faithful

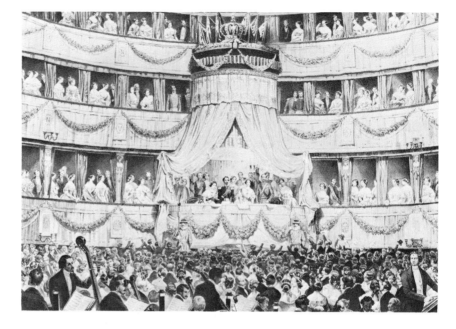

A gala evening at the
Royal Opera House,
Covent Garden, in honour
of the State Visit of
Napoleon III and Empress
Eugénie in 1855

towards us'. Just how well she used the warmth of her own family to make
visiting Heads of State feel welcome is clear from a letter to her uncle, the
King of the Belgians, following visits from the Czar of Russia and the King
of Saxony in 1844.

How many different Princes have we not gone the same round with!! The children
are much admired by the *Sovereigns* – (how *grand* this sounds!) – and Alice allowed
the Emperor to take her in his arms and kissed him de son propre accord. We are
always so thankful that they are *not* shy. Both the Emepror and the King are *quite*
enchanted with Windsor.

Nowadays few State visits are made by reigning monarchs. State are
usually represented by their Presidents. Yet the pageantry of a royal
welcome and the honour of an invitation from the Queen, together with the
Queen's undoubted success in making those who arrive on State visits feel
personally welcomed, cannot be overestimated.

State visits between France and Britain during the time of Queen
Victoria and Edward VII were an important factor in bringing about the
entente cordiale after a history of hostility stretching back to the time of the
Norman Conquest and reaching its peak at the battle of Waterloo in 1815.
Today, after being allies through two World Wars, we are accustomed to
think of France as a friend rather than an enemy but tensions still exist
because of our different expectations from the Common Market. In 1976
President Giscard d'Estaing of France paid a State visit to this country
when it was felt that his attitude to Britain was rather defensive. Yet the

visit, during which the Queen made him a present of a gun-dog, for they share an interest in field sports, was a resounding success. It was generally agreed that much of the credit for this belonged to the Queen herself. The Paris correspondent of the *Evening Standard* wrote, 'If the visit can be pronounced an outstanding success which, for the time being at any rate, has transformed Anglo-French relations, then the credit must go almost entirely to the Queen.' The former Labour MP Woodrow Wyatt pointed out the part which ceremonial and pageantry played in achieving that success:

It would not have been quite the same if the President and the Queen had ridden on bicycles down the Mall instead of in a gorgeous carriage. At a time when so much in Britain has declined the value of the Monarchy to us has actually increased.

The ritual surrounding a State visit does not vary greatly. Usually visitors arrive by air at Gatwick airport where there is a Guard of Honour provided by the RAF. The visitor is then taken by a special train to Victoria Station. Here the Queen waits to greet him or her and the State visit formally begins. This is marked by the firing of a Royal Gun Salute as the visitor steps on to the red carpet. The station is transformed for the occasion with flags and bunting of various kinds which make it almost unrecognizable, while music provided by military bands adds to the air of festivity. Here a second Guard of Honour found from The Guards Division is lined up for inspection by the distinguished visitor.

The next stage is a State drive along the processional route, which has also been decorated with flags and which is lined with soldiers. The visitor is taken either for a State Banquet at the Guildhall or directly back to Buckingham Palace where a State Banquet may be held in the Ball Room. The Queen, the visiting Head of State, and any other members of the Royal Family travel in open carriages with an Escort of the Household Cavalry. In the past important visitors were usually transported by water along the Thames to whichever royal palace they were being entertained at – the old Palaces of Westminster, Greenwich, Windsor, and Hampton Court are all accessible from the river – so the Queen's Barge-master and Watermen are 'boxmen' on some carriages in the Procession, just as they are in the procession for the State Opening of Parliament.

On arrival at the Grand Entrance of Buckingham Palace the Queen and her visitor are greeted by yet another Guard of Honour from the Guards Division and the National Anthems of both countries are played. The steps of the Palace are lined by dismounted Troopers of the Household Cavalry, one of the few occasions when they parade dismounted. In the Palace itself the two Royal Bodyguards, the Honourable Corps of Gentlemen at Arms and the Yeomen of the Guard are on duty, both bodies wearing their distinctive ceremonial uniforms. Inside the Palace the

Queen introduces the visiting Head of State to the members of her household.

If the State visit is to begin at Windsor the visitor flies in to Heathrow airport and drives to the Home Park, where the Queen and her family are waiting to greet him or her in a Pavilion complete with dais and red carpet. There is a Guard of Honour to inspect and, as in London, a Royal Gun Salute is fired by men of the King's Troop, Royal Horse Artillery.

The Queen arrives at the Pavilion in her Rolls Royce but the return to the Castle takes the traditional form of a carriage drive with an Escort of Household Cavalry. The streets of Windsor are decorated for the occasion by the local council. Once at the Castle the Mounted Band of the Household Cavalry, the King's Troop, and the 116 men who make up the Sovereign's Escort of the Household Cavalry rank past in the quadrangle while the Guard of Honour and a Guards Band is formed up on the lawn in the centre. It is a magnificent display of military pageantry in a fairy tale setting which must surely flatter the self-esteem of any visitor.

Those Heads of State who arrive in Scotland to begin their visits are greeted by the Queen in Charlotte Square. This is followed by a State Drive in open carriages or the Scottish State Coach along a processional route lined with soldiers and police and decorated as usual with flags, to the Palace of Holyroodhouse. The Sovereign's Escort used to be provided by a Scottish Regiment, the Royal Scots Greys. However, this is now a mechanized regiment, which, unliked the mechanized regiments of The Household Division, The Life Guards, and The Blues and Royals, no longer keeps a ceremonial unit. The Royal Scots Greys last escorted the Queen in 1953 when she paid her own State visit to Scotland after her Coronation. Nowadays a Sovereign's Escort in Scotland is provided by the Household Cavalry. However, when the Procession reaches Holyroodhouse a Guard of Honour from one of the Scottish Regiments is formed up and the Queen's Bodyguard for Scotland – the Royal Company of Archers – provide a uniquely Scottish ingredient in their green uniforms and distinctive bonnets decorated with eagle feathers.

Much of the entertainment provided for a Head of State is informal, as it was in Queen Victoria's time. The object is to fête the visitor but also make him or her feel relaxed and at home in this country. In his diary Greville describes a typical programme for a visitor in Victoria's day, in this case the Emperor of Russia.

He immediately visited all the Royal Family, and the Duke of Wellington. . . . On Monday he went to Windsor, Tuesday to Ascot, Wednesday they gave him a Review. . . . The sight was pretty glorious weather, 3,000 or 4,000 Guards, Horse, Foot and Artillery in the Park, the Queen en caleche with a brilliant suite. . . . On Thursday they went to Ascot again, where they were received very well by a dense multitude. On Friday to London where they gave him a . . . party at the Palace. On Saturday a

Opposite top: The King's Troop, the Royal Horse Artillery, firing a Gun Salute in Hyde Park

Opposite, bottom: The Charter for the Investiture of Prince Charles, son of James I, as Prince of Wales in 1616. This followed the lines laid down by the first Charter of 1343 when the Black Prince was created Prince of Wales by his father, Edward III

Overleaf, top: The Crown of Robert the Bruce, one of the Honours of Scotland (the Scottish Crown Jewels)

Overleaf, bottom left: The Lord Lyon in the Thistle Ceremony Procession in Edinburgh

Overleaf, bottom right: The Queen and Prince Edward at Badminton Horse Trials – no different from any of the other spectators

breakfast at Chiswick, a beautiful fête and perfectly successful. Everything that was distinguished in London was collected to see and be seen by the Emperor. At the Opera, which was crowded from top to bottom, he was very well received.

A visiting Head of State 140 years later might expect a very similar programme. Distinguished visitors who arrive in June are usually taken to Ascot, and some of them are invested with the Order of the Garter, as an additional mark of esteem, at the beginning of Ascot Week. A visit to the Royal Opera House at Covent Garden is still a likely part of the entertainment. Such a gala evening is planned months ahead and the audience wears evening dress, complete with decorations, and tiaras for the women. The Queen's Bodyguard, the Yeomen of the Guard, are present in ceremonial uniform and for that one evening the doormen wear footmen's uniform, including a wig.

A State visit combines both informal and semi-formal entertainments, a relaxed stroll round the gardens of Buckingham Palace with the Queen or a glittering night at the Opera. The most formal of the entertainments provided is the State Banquet.

State Banquets may be held in the Ball Room of Buckingham Palace, or in St George's Hall, Windsor. Occasionally, as for the State visit of King Olav v of Norway in 1962, a State Banquet is held at the Palace of Holyroodhouse. Whatever the venue the procedure is usually more or less the same. The Queen and the other women wear evening dress with tiaras. The men may wear dress uniform or black tail coats. Some of the men, Prince Philip usually one of them, wear Court dress which consists of a black tail coat worn with knee breeches and black stockings. With Court dress those, like Prince Philip, who are Knights of the Garter, wear the Garter below the left knee. The Queen usually wears an Order given to her by the Head of State whom she is entertaining.

The guests go two by two in formal procession into the meal. The Queen leads this with her guest, if it is a man, or the husband of her guest when, as in the State visit of the Danish Queen Margrethe II, the Head of State is a woman. The Lord Chamberlain and the Lord Steward, each carrying a white wand, walk in front of the procession. The Queen sits in the middle of a horse-shoe shaped table and her guests are seated in order of precedence. Great care is taken with the floral decorations and with the table setting. The cutlery and dinner service used are of silver-gilt. There are many priceless dinner services in the royal collection which may be brought out for such an occasion.

At a State Banquet the footmen wear eighteenth-century style livery of scarlet and gold. Until the reign of Elizabeth II it was customary for them

Previous page: Queen Elizabeth arriving at St Paul's Cathedral in the Great State Coach for the Silver Jubilee Service in 1977. (This was the first time the coach had been used since her Coronation)

Opposite: The Prince and Princess of Wales returning to Buckingham Palace after their wedding in St Paul's Cathedral

to wear their hair powdered as well. The Foot Guards provide an orchestra which plays throughout the meal and at the conclusion twelve pipers from the Scots Guards come in and play while they march round the table. This custom originated with Queen Victoria who was charmed by all aspects of Scottish life and culture.

In addition to the State Banquet given by the Queen a visiting Head of State is entertained to another State Banquet given by the Lord Mayor of London. Occasionally, though less often these days because of the problems created by a carriage procession through the City, this takes the form of a luncheon. More often it is an evening Banquet and the visitor, who has been entertained by the best that royal ceremonial has to offer, is given a taste of the pageantry of the City of London. The Banquet is held at the Guildhall. The Lord Mayor, accompanied by his Sword Bearer and Mace Bearer, the Sheriffs, and the City Remembrancer greets the Head of State. A Guard of Honour is formed by the Company of Pikeman and Musketeers, the ceremonial group within the Honourable Artillery Company which provides the Lord Mayor's Bodyguard and the Sovereign's Escort in the City (see p. 76).

During the reception in the Library a brief meeting of the Court of Aldermen is held to propose and second the motion that the guest should receive an address of welcome. This formality over, the Procession, heralded by a fanfare from the State Trumpeters, is led into the Great Hall of the Guildhall where the Banquet is held.

Date **Usually there are two State visits a year. The Court and Social pages of 'The Times' and 'Daily Telegraph' and the Today's Events column in 'The Times' publish details.**
Time **Times may vary but generally a Head of State arrives at Victoria Station at 12.45 p.m.**
Place **Most State visits begin at Victoria Station. Members of the public are not allowed inside the station but those who have places outside the station entrance will see the Guard of Honour and the Procession as it sets out for Buckingham Palace or the Guildhall. Arrive by 10.30 a.m. for a key position.**

The route of the Procession will vary according to the destination. The British Tourist Authority (see p. 176) should have details of the route in advance. Times of State Banquets at the Guildhall are given in the Press in advance. To watch the arrival of the Queen and her guests it is best to be outside the Guildhall about two hours beforehand. Those who wait outside the Guildhall before a lunchtime banquet will also see the State procession arrive.

If the visiting Head of State is to be greeted by the Queen at Windsor details of times will appear beforehand in the Press. Members of the public are not allowed close enough to the Pavilion in the Home Park to witness the Head of State's arrival but may stand along the processional route. This usually makes its way through the streets of Windsor along the Long Walk and into the Castle through the George IV Gateway. Members of the public are not allowed in to see the rank past in the Quadrangle.

If a visiting Head of State is arriving in Scotland the Queen will greet him at Charlotte Square. Times are given in the Press. A State Procession travels through the streets of Edinburgh and along the historic 'Royal Mile' to Holyroodhouse. Members of the public are not allowed into Holyroodhouse while the Queen is in residence.

State Visits and Banquets / Royal Ascot

Royal Ascot

The Royal Ascot Race Meeting is not a ceremonial occasion in the same sense as Trooping the Colour or the State Opening of Parliament. It does not involve military display, the heralds or the Church. Yet because it gives so many people the chance to see the Queen at close quarters, especially during the semi-formal carriage procession along the course, it has become one of the Royal Family's most familiar rituals.

Horse racing seems to have been a popular sport with many British monarchs and Elizabeth II is as keen as any of them. Not only does she own and race horses; she also breeds them and has a stud farm at Sandringham. Royal Ascot is therefore an annual engagement which perhaps more than any of her other commitments is pure pleasure. During Ascot Week the Queen is in residence at Windsor Castle where she entertains a large house party made up mostly of racing enthusiasts like herself, although visiting Heads of State sometimes stay during Ascot Week.

Ascot is called Royal Ascot because the Sovereign owns the land on which the course is built, although the Queen takes no revenue from it. Charles II, whose ruin, according to the Bishop of Salisbury, 'was occasioned chiefly by his delivering himself up at his first coming over to a mad range of pleasure', had founded an annual race meeting at Datchet Mead.

His niece, Queen Anne, who was extremely fond of riding, hunting and horse racing, transferred this annual event to Ascot which is more conveniently placed to Windsor Castle. She popularized the event and gave both the Queen's Plate and a 100 guinea prize. She also inaugurated the custom of a carriage procession from Windsor Castle to the race course when she arrived for the first meeting on 11 August 1711. George IV a hundred years later began the custom of continuing the drive along the race course itself to the royal box. He drove in a coach and four attended by the Master of the Buckhounds. It was George IV's unfulfilled ambition to win the cup at Ascot and he bought many expensive horses in the attempt.

The ride down the course became an occasion when the crowd could show its enthusiasm or otherwise for their Sovereign. Greville tells us that

157

The traditional arrival by carriage of the royal party at Ascot, seen here in 1891

when William IV drove down the course in 1831 'The reception was strikingly cold and indifferent, not half so good as that which the late King used to receive'. Queen Victoria had the unpleasant experience of being hissed by several Tory ladies who disliked her preference for Whig politicians. No one however could doubt the popularity of her son, the Prince of Wales, who was in his element among the racing set. His progress along the course each afternoon was a noisy and exuberant display which included the Master of the Buckhounds, the royal huntsman, and an assortment of whippers in, footmen, postilions, and park keepers.

The carriage procession along the race course is now a much more formal and elegant affair. The Queen does not drive in a carriage all the way from Windsor. She and her party arrive at Ascot by car and transfer to the Ascot landaus for the Procession up the course. The landaus are kept at Windsor where they are also used to carry the royal party back from the Garter service. They are of the type known as postilion landaus. This is because there is no driver's box so each pair of horses require a postilion rider. They are lighter than the semi-state landaus and have basketwork sides. The first landau in the Procession, which carries the Queen, Prince Philip, the Master of the Queen's Horse, and perhaps a visiting Head of State, is drawn by four greys, preceded by two outriders, also on greys. Each of the others is drawn by four bays with one outrider mounted on a bay. The Queen Mother generally travels in the second carriage.

The Queen attends all the races, which she watches from the royal box. The Ascot Gold Cup which was first offered by George III in 1807 stays with her until it is won on the third day.

Date **Usually the Wednesday, Thursday, Friday and Saturday of the third week in June.**

Time **The Royal Procession along the course takes place at 2.00 p.m.**

When to arrive **The Ascot Office advise you to arrive no later than mid-day because of parking difficulties. It is advisable to travel without a car if possible.**

Tickets **Can be bought at Ascot race course or by ringing in advance (see p. 176).**

Tickets for the Royal Enclosure **The Royal Enclosure is the most exciting place to be at Ascot. In 1968 it was made permissible to wear lounge suits but this proved unpopular and formal wear is still customary. The announcement in 'The Times' states that ladies will wear formal day dress with hats, gentlemen morning dress or service dress. Anyone except ex-convicts or undischarged bankrupts can apply to be on the list for tickets to the Royal Enclosure. Divorced people have been admitted since 1955. New applicants must be sponsored by someone who is already on the Royal Enclosure list. (Visitors from overseas should apply to their Ambassador or High Commissioner.) Applications for admission to the Royal Ascot Enclosure should be made between 1 January and 30 April (see p. 176). Children under the age of ten are not admitted. Children aged ten to fifteen are admitted on the Friday only.**

Informal Occasions

Much of Britain's ceremonial is popular with the crowds simply because it offers a chance to see the Queen or close members of her family. For the same reason occasions such as Her Majesty's arrival at a Royal Film Première or the Commonwealth Observance Service at Westminster Abbey attract large numbers although there is no ceremonial involved at all. These 'informal' occasions do nevertheless have a certain formality to them because of the organization which is involved in even the simplest of the Queen's engagements.

The organization of the Queen's programme, both the State ceremonial and more routine events, is the responsibility of various officials and departments of the Royal Household. In the early Middle Ages, when the king's household and the government were one and the same thing, many posts of great responsibility developed. Most of them exist today with archaic sounding titles which are still a reminder of their quasi-domestic origin. Seven of these eventually became almost totally governmental positions: the Lord High Steward, the Lord Chancellor, the Lord President of the Council, the Lord Privy Seal, the Lord Great Chamberlain, the Lord High Constable and the Earl Marshal. Of these the Lord Chancellor, the Lord President of the Council, and the Lord Privy Seal are still important political appointments. The Lord High Steward, the Lord Great Chamberlain, and the Lord High Constable are now purely ceremonial appointments although the honour of the position is still very great. Nowadays the Lord High Steward and the Lord High Constable are created for the day of the Coronation only.

The Earl Marshal of England is the only one of the seven Great Officers of State who fulfils a function similar to that of his medieval namesake. He has a unique position – not part of the government as such nor involved in the day to day running of the Royal Household. He is responsible for the organization and administration of State ceremonies. In this job he is assisted by the heralds for he is Head of the College of Arms. Ceremonies for which the Earl Marshal is responsible include the Coronation, the Investiture of the Prince of Wales, State funerals, and the State Opening of Parliament. The office is an hereditary one and the Earl Marshal of England since 1672 has always been the Duke of Norfolk.

However, the Queen and members of the Royal Family are involved in much ceremonial which is not strictly State ceremonial. These royal ceremonies, like the Epiphany service, as well as informal engagements, are the direct responsibility of the Royal Household. The three Great Officers of the Household in order of seniority are: the Lord Chamberlain, the Lord Steward, and the Master of the Horse. Of these the Lord Steward is now an almost totally ceremonial office, with no responsibility for any administration, although at one time the staff of the royal palaces came under his control. At State Banquets he presents guests to the Sovereign for he is theoretically responsible for the organization of these functions, a job which is now undertaken by the Master of the Household who is a professional administrator.

The Master of the Horse, as might be expected, is the Officer who is theoretically responsible for road transport arrangements. This office is also an honorary one. In his ceremonial capacity the Master of the Horse rides in the Procession at the Coronation, Trooping the Colour, and the Sovereign's funeral. His past importance can be judged by the fact that he comes in the second carriage at the State Opening of Parliament and accompanies an unmarried Sovereign in the coach to his or her Coronation. Although, as with a recent holder of the office, the Duke of Beaufort, someone with a genuine interest in horses or any of the forms of transport used by the Royal Family today may have a great deal of influence, the actual day to day administration of all the Royal Household's road transport problems, at home and abroad, is the responsibility of the Crown Equerry. All the carriages in the royal mews are under his control and all the royal motor cars. Transport of the Royal Family to any event from a visit to a hospital to a royal wedding is his responsibility.

Even busier than the office of the Master of the Horse is the office of the

Lord Chamberlain, and even busier than the Crown Equerry is the Comptroller of the Lord Chamberlain's office who handles the day to day arrangements.

The Lord Chamberlain is the senior of the three Great Officers of State, and he has resonsibility for all the Sovereign's public engagements as well as for many other matters like the issue of Royal Warrants and the appointment of the Poet Laureate. The Lord Chamberlain himself performs the many ceremonial functions which are part of his office. The administration of ceremonial occasions is handled by his Comptroller and Assistant Comptroller, usually former army officers, together with a small staff. Among the events they organize are the Investitures at Buckingham Palace, the annual Garden Parties, royal weddings, and State visits from abroad. It is their job to see that the Queen and her family are in the right place at the right time for all the ceremonies, including State ceremonies. They also oversee the administration of the royal palaces and the royal art collections.

The Queen's more informal engagements, such as opening the Barbican Centre, are organized by the Queen's Private Secretary. He is responsible for planning her diary, overseeing her constitutional duties and for the precise planning of visits overseas. The Royal Household is rightly proud of its reputation for meticulous forward planning and impeccable timing, all of it the result of close attention to detail. It is not surprising therefore that even the most informal royal occasion has an element of ceremonial and ritual about it which leaves the people who attend it with the sense of having taken part in a very special event.

The Court and Social pages of 'The Times' and 'Daily Telegraph' carry details of future engagements of the Queen and the Royal Family. They also carry full details after events such as State visits. Some engagements, such as the Queen's attendance at the Commonwealth Observance Ceremony at Westminster Abbey, are announced months in advance.

The 'Today's Events' section on the back page of 'The Times' carries details of the Queen's engagements for that particular day.

The local Press carries details of the Queen's visits to particular areas.

Below is a small selection of the Royal Family's hundreds of informal engagements throughout the year.

PALACE GARDEN PARTIES

There are usually four Garden Parties a year, three at Buckingham Palace and one at Holyroodhouse Palace in Edinburgh. When in 1958 the Queen decided to end the custom of Courts or Presentation parties at which debutantes were formally introduced to her the number of Garden Parties

Queen Mary at a
Holyroodhouse garden
party in 1927

was increased to compensate. About 8,000 people attend each one and not only does this give over 30,000 people the chance of an invitation from the Queen each year but enables Her Majesty to reward public service and outstanding contributions to the community in a way which the former Presentation parties did not.

Admission is by invitation only. The invitations are handled by a special section of the Lord Chamberlain's Office. Extra staff are taken on for about six months just to cope with the work arising from the Garden Parties and their extended stay has earned them the nickname of the 'permanent temporaries'.

Those who have accepted invitations receive tickets well in advance and special stickers for the windscreens of their cars. Many people prefer to arrive by public transport because of the terrible traffic jams which result from the convergence of 8,000 people on the Palace in one afternoon. The invitations offer the alternative of morning dress, uniform, or lounge suits and many people take the opportunity to dress up.

One of the characteristics of these parties is the queues, first to hand in invitations and then to get from the Bow Room into the garden itself. Once in the Palace garden the sense of over-crowding disappears as there are thirty-nine acres in which to wander. Uniformed Yeomen of the Guard, Gentlemen at Arms, and Gentlemen Ushers are responsible for overseeing the guests and bringing some of them forward to have a few words with the Queen.

At four o'clock the National Anthem is played by one of the military bands which provides music from Gilbert and Sullivan, light opera, and musicals throughout the afternoon.

The Queen, the Duke of Edinburgh, and any other members of the

The Queen at a recent
Buckingham Palace garden
party where she was
hostess to about 7,000
people

Royal Family emerge from the Palace and make their way slowly towards
the royal tent. The Lord Chamberlain walks beside the Queen and the
other members of the Royal Family take separate routes so that they
come into contact with as many people as possible. The Gentlemen Ushers
bring forward several people at random for a few minutes' conversation
with the Queen or her family. The Queen then has tea in the royal tent
(there is also a separate tent for diplomats and another for ordinary
visitors). The food offered consists of sandwiches, scones, cake, and
Indian tea. Until they became too expensive strawberries and cream used
to be offered. After tea the Queen meets distinguished Commonwealth
visitors before beginning a slow progress back to the Palace. At 5 o'clock
once she has gone back inside there is a tremendous crush as the 8,000
guests all try to leave at once!

Although the chances of getting trodden on are greater than at most
royal occasions, and although it may be a strain even to catch a glimpse of
the Queen, a Royal Garden Party is an honour and a thrill which no one
given the opportunity of attending should miss.

ROYAL FILM PERFORMANCE, ODEON, LEICESTER SQUARE
ROYAL COMMAND PERFORMANCE, DRURY LANE THEATRE OR
LONDON PALLADIUM

There is no fixed date for either of these occasions but the Royal Film
Performance generally takes place in March and the Command Performance in November. The royal party arrives at 7.30 p.m. and to see them it is
advisable to be in position by about 5.30 p.m.

Dates of both performances are given in advance in the Press. Tickets for the Royal Film Performance are sometimes advertised beforehand. Tickets for either occasion are usually expensive as the proceeds go to charity.

THE CHELSEA FLOWER SHOW

The Queen always attends the Chelsea Flower Show on the day before the Show officially opens unless she is travelling abroad. She generally arrives at about 4 p.m.

Tickets for the first day of the show, which is held by the Royal Horticultural Society, are available to members only. There are no membership restrictions; to belong you simply need to pay the subscription. The Society's offices are in Vincent Square, London S.W.1. The Chelsea Flower Show takes place at the Royal Hospital Grounds, Chelsea, London S.W.3. There is no fixed date but it is usually some time in late May.

BADMINTON HORSE TRIALS   DERBY DAY, EPSOM

The Queen and members of the Royal Family can often be seen at well known equestrian events, notably the Derby which is held in June and the Badminton Horse Trials which are held in April. Times and details of these events, including current ticket prices, may be written for in advance (see p. 176).

BRAEMAR, THE ROYAL HIGHLAND GATHERING

This takes place annually in the Princess Royal Park near Balmoral, usually in the first week in September. It was instituted by the Braemar Highland Society in the 1830s and became a royal event with the patronage of Queen Victoria after she and Prince Albert bought nearby Balmoral. It is an occasion which the Queen nearly always attends and there is usually at least one member of the Royal Family present. There are all the events of a traditional Highland Games, including putting the stone, throwing the hammer, wrestling, and tossing the caber. There are also bands, bagpipes, and displays of Scottish dancing.

Admission is by ticket only (see p. 176). There is usually a heavy demand for tickets and it is advisable to book early in the year. Times of the Games vary and will be sent with your tickets.

WALKABOUTS

This expression to describe the Queen's informal walks through the crowds was first coined during one of her visits to Australia. (A walkabout is an expression used when aborigines wander off by themselves into the bush.) In the 1960s, when the Royal Family appeared to be making extra efforts to make themselves more available and well-known to the public, these 'walkabouts' which had proved such a popular feature of the Queen's visits abroad were incorporated into many of her itineraries at home as well. They give the Queen a chance to chat informally, if only briefly, with a wide cross section of the people, and already a tradition has grown up of offering small posies of flowers which are often so numerous that the Queen's Lady in Waiting looks quite weighed down with them.

The Duke of Edinburgh's ability to talk easily with most people on many subjects has made him particularly adept at this type of occasion. The Prince of Wales too has adapted easily to this new style of royal visit and the Princess of Wales now receives almost as many posies as the Queen, if not more. Perhaps the most successful walkabouts of all were the ones which the Queen went on during her Silver Jubilee year in 1977. These took place not just in London, where the route she took is marked by special plaques in the pavement, but also on her tours around the United Kingdom (except in Belfast where security was too tight) and in the Commonwealth.

The Queen talking to enthusiastic crowds in the City of London during a Silver Jubilee walkabout, June 1977

Lady Diana Spencer shortly before her marriage, chatting to another member of the crowd

Even though walkabouts are relatively informal and now feature in most of the Queen's visits to various towns they are not totally free and easy. A specific route is laid down, usually roped off, so that the Queen can make her way easily through the crowds.

Details of the route for a royal walkabout are generally given in the local Press of the area the Queen is visiting. When a walkabout is part of a more formal occasion, such as the Silver Jubilee celebrations or a State visit abroad, the route is given in the official programme. As with every occasion those who arrive in good time get the best view and in this case the chance of speaking to the Queen.

Jubilees

Jubilees are a relatively novel type of celebration. Elizabeth II's Silver Jubilee was only the second time such an anniversary had been celebrated although since the Conquest thirteen Sovereigns have reigned for twenty-five years or more.

The first officially celebrated Jubilee was the Golden Jubilee in 1810 of George III. The King himself was by this stage too ill and mentally unstable to attend the festivities himself. Yet by that time he had been on the throne for so long that in spite of his disabilities, which meant that he was no longer seen in public, the people retained an affection for him as an apparently permanent feature in their lives.

George III's Golden Jubilee celebrations were on a very small scale. There was a small fête with a celebratory roasted ox in the grounds of Windsor Castle. (This was later commemorated by an obelisk.) At the end of the day there was a firework display, a form of festivity which has become a feature of all royal jubilee celebrations.

Queen Victoria reigned even longer than George III, and like him had come to seem like a permanent fixture to her subjects. She did not celebrate a Silver Jubilee in 1862, not just because it was only a year after the death of Prince Albert and any form of celebration seemed like a betrayal to her, but also simply because it was not a custom to celebrate an anniversary of twenty-five years.

The occasion of Victoria's Golden Jubilee was the event which finally jolted her back into public life after twenty-five years of semi-seclusion. At the Prince of Wales's insistence she sanctioned the idea of a full-scale Jubilee celebration. The entire year was tied up with Jubilee festivities, for which large numbers of souvenirs and medals, which are now an integral part of any Jubilee, were made. Among the gestures made for the Jubilee was the remission of many prison sentences both at home and in the Empire.

The actual anniversary of Victoria's accession to the throne, 20 June, was one of the many brilliantly hot days enjoyed that summer which gave rise to the expression 'Queen's weather'. The Thanksgiving Service took place in Westminster Abbey on 21 June, and there was a magnificent procession to and from the church. The Queen herself rode in an open landau drawn by six cream horses and with an escort of Indian cavalry, for as well as being Queen of England she was also proud of her title Empress of India. Among the glitter of the foreign royalty and of her extensive family the Queen stood out because of the simplicity of her own dress. She had refused to wear her crown and carry the other regalia, preferring a simple white, lace-edged bonnet with discreetly sparkling diamonds. Such simplicity was probably the only thing which could have distinguished her so effectively, for the many splendidly robed and bejewelled representatives from the Empire and European royal families created an overwhelmingly magnificent sight which the waiting crowds loudly approved.

Among the other features of Victoria's Golden Jubilee which set the pattern for future Jubilees were a review of the Army at Aldershot and of the Navy at Spithead, visits to many provincial cities such as Birmingham, street parties, garden parties at the Palace, dinners, banquets, receptions, and beacons lit right across the country.

It was a tiring, if exhilarating, schedule for a lady of sixty-seven and it is not surprising that for her Diamond Jubilee in 1897 Queen Victoria preferred to limit some of the celebrations. The ten years since her Golden Jubilee had seen a great upsurge in the Queen's popularity, both because she herself had become less of a recluse and because of the increasing imperial power of Britain for which the Queen was the symbol. The date chosen for the main celebration was 22 June, and the sun shone as brilliantly as it had done ten years earlier. Once again there was a triumphal procession through the streets of London, which had been lavishly decorated by those who lived in them.

Because it had been decided to invite Prime Ministers rather than crowned Heads of State, Kaiser Wilhelm, her grandson, who had been so popular when he rode in the Golden Jubilee Procession, was absent. This was fortunate because by that time he was regarded with intense dislike by the British people. The demonstration of affection from the crowds was deafening and Queen Victoria found it so moving that she was seen to cry. That evening she wrote in her journal, 'No-one ever, I believe, has met with such an ovation as was given to me, passing through those six miles of streets including Constitution Hill. The crowds were quite indescribable, and their enthusiasm truly marvellous and deeply touching. The cheering was quite deafening, and every face seemed to be filled with real joy.'

The procession went this time to St Paul's Cathedral, for Westminster Abbey was too small for the scale of the service to which representatives from countries all over the world had been invited. Because of the Queen's age and increasing infirmity the service was kept brief. Her Majesty, however, remained throughout in her carriage at the steps of St Paul's for her rheumatism made the ascent into the Cathedral itself an impossibility and she still recalled with horror the immense heat in the Abbey during her Golden Jubilee Service.

The remaining celebrations in 1897 were similar to those of a decade earlier except that they were marked by an even greater level of enthusiasm – more beacons, more souvenirs, more decorations, and more loyal crowds.

In addition the great technological achievements of the past sixty years was plainly in evidence, not just in the gas and electric street lighting which decorated the streets, but in the method used by the Queen to inaugurate the celebrations. 'I touched an electric button, by which I started a message which was telegraphed throughout the whole Empire. It was the following: "From my heart I thank my beloved people. May God bless them!"'

It was plain from the many messages she received in her turn that her arch-enemy, Mr Gladstone's, remark that he wished she might celebrate her Diamond Jubilee by abdicating, did not reflect the feelings of Queen Victoria's subjects, either at home or in the Empire.

Edward VII was sixty when he succeeded his mother in 1901 and he reigned for a mere nine years. His own son, George V, reigned for just over twenty-five years and it was decided to hold a special Silver Jubilee to celebrate them. His reign, which had covered the First World War and the terrible economic depression of the thirties, was certainly not as splendid as his grandmother's. Yet George V's straightforward personality and sense of fair play had made him surprisingly popular with the people and the monarchy had survived some of its most precarious years, an achievement which even Edward VII would not have taken for granted. He once introduced his son only half in jest as 'the last King of England'.

For all his restricted experience of anything outside his own class, George V had been ready to see every point of view. When, during the General Strike of 1926, a wealthy mine-owner had called the striking mineworkers a 'damned lot of revolutionaries' George V's response had been 'Try living on their wages before you judge them'. When, on one of the many visits he made around the country to celebrate his Jubilee year, the King visited the East End of London, he was startled by the warmth of his reception, rather as Queen Victoria had been by hers. 'I'd no idea they felt like that about me. I am beginning to think they like me for myself.' Jubilee Day itself, 6 May, was the sort of hot sunny day which had helped make Queen Victoria's Jubilees so memorable. The Thanksgiving Service was held in St Paul's Cathedral and that evening a new aspect of Jubilees, the monarch's broadcast to the nation, was added to the traditions that were growing up around this comparatively new type of festival. George V had already begun the habit of making a Christmas broadcast each year. This time he spoke at the end of what had been an emotional occasion for both the King and Queen and the crowds who came to see them.

At the close of this memorable day, I must speak to my people everywhere. How can I express what is in my heart? I thank you from the depths of our hearts for all the loyalty – and may I say so? – the love, with which this day and always you have surrounded us. I dedicate myself anew to your service for all the years that may still be given me.

George v and Queen Mary
driving along Commercial
Road during his successful
Silver Jubilee visit to the
East End of London, 1935

In 1935 a Silver Jubilee Trust had been started by public subscription
to be used for projects concerned with the youth of the country. This
method of tapping Jubilee enthusiasm for a worthy cause was repeated for
Elizabeth ii's Silver Jubilee in 1977. The 1935 fund had been headed by
Edward, Prince of Wales, soon to become Edward viii. The Chairman of
the 1977 Silver Jubilee Appeal was Prince Charles, the present Prince of
Wales. The fund, which quickly reached an astonishing £16 million, is to
be used, at the Queen's request, 'to help young people help others'. Because
of the similarity of their aims the 1935 and 1977 Trusts were amalgamated
and as a result the committee has £1 million a year to give in grants to
worthwhile projects. This precedent of using the goodwill which grows
up around a Jubilee and putting it to practical and long term use is one
which will surely be followed when any other Jubilee is celebrated.

In other ways the Queen's Silver Jubilee incorporated all the elements of
previous festivities. The focus of the year was the Thanksgiving Service
which was held in St Paul's Cathedral. The Service, and the Procession in
which the Queen rode in the gold State Coach used for her Coronation,
were participated in by more people than ever before because of television.
Yet despite the success of using modern technology to communicate more
widely and effectively, one of the most spectacular features of the Jubilee
was the chain of beacons which was lit across the country, a technique of
communication which had been used at the time of the Armada nearly 400
years before. Although the June of 1977 failed to provide the 'Queen's
weather' which had enhanced the Jubilees of the Queen's predecessors the
enthusiasm and spontaneity of the rejoicing seemed unimpaired. As
nearly a quarter of a million people surged round Buckingham Palace on

For the first time since her Coronation the Great State Coach was used in the Queen's Silver Jubilee celebrations in 1977, here on its way to St Paul's

7 June, shouting 'We Want the Queen', there seemed no doubt that royalty together with its rituals new and old, would be a living and integral part of Britain and the Commonwealth for as far into the future as anyone could possibly predict.

Annual Events

DATE	EVENT	PLACE
6 January	Epiphany Service	Chapel Royal, St James's Palace
6 February	Royal Gun Salute for anniversary of Queen's Accession	Hyde Park, twelve noon and the Tower of London, 1.00 p.m.
1 March (or nearest Sunday)	St David's Day: leeks given to Welsh Guards	Wherever 1st Battalion Welsh Guards are stationed
17 March	St Patrick's Day: shamrocks given to Irish Guards	Wherever 1st Battalion Irish Guards are stationed
Late March. No fixed date, see Press	Royal Film Performance	Odeon Cinema, Leicester Square
Thursday before Good Friday	Royal Maundy Distribution	Westminster Abbey or cathedral or church in major town or city
3 days, mid-April, see Press	Badminton Horse Trials	Badminton, Avon
21 April	Royal Gun Salute for Queen's Birthday	Hyde Park and the Tower of London
Early May. Check with Windsor Tourist Authority	Royal Mausoleum open to public	Frogmore, Windsor
May for one week. See Press	General Assembly of Church of Scotland Inaugural Service	St Giles's Cathedral, Edinburgh
3 days, late May. No fixed date, see Press	Chelsea Flower Show	Royal Hospital Grounds, Chelsea, SW3
Late May (around 26), see Press	Holyroodhouse Garden Party	Holyroodhouse, Edinburgh
29 May (on or near)	Founder's Day	Royal Hospital, Chelsea
Late May/early June, see Press	Beating Retreat	Horse Guards Parade
2 June	Royal Gun Salute for Queen's Coronation	Hyde Park and the Tower of London
1st or 2nd Saturday in June (usually). No fixed date, see Press	The Queen's Birthday Parade – Trooping the Colour	Horse Guards Parade
As above, 11.00 a.m.	Royal Gun Salute for Official Birthday	Hyde Park and the Tower of London
Early June	Derby Day	Epsom Race Course

Annual Events	10 June	Royal Gun Salute for Duke of Edinburgh's Birthday	Hyde Park and the Tower of London
	Mid-June	Royal Ascot	Ascot Race Course
	Mid-June, Monday of Ascot Week	Garter Ceremony	Windsor Castle
	Last two weeks in July	Royal Tournament	Earl's Court, SW5
	Last week in July	Sovereign's Parade	Royal Military Academy, Sandhurst
	Mid- to late July	Garden Parties	Buckingham Palace
	4 August	Royal Gun Salute for Queen Mother's Birthday	Hyde Park and the Tower of London
	1st week in September	Braemar: Royal Highland Gathering	Princess Royal Park, Balmoral
	Late October/ early November	State Opening of Parliament	Houses of Parliament
	As above	Royal Gun Salute for State Opening	Hyde Park
	2nd Saturday in November	Lord Mayor's Show	Route – Guildhall to Royal Courts of Justice, via the Mansion House
	11 November or nearest Sunday	Remembrance Sunday – Cenotaph Ceremony	Cenotaph, Whitehall
	As above, 11.00 a.m.	Gun Salute for Remembrance Sunday	Horse Guards Parade
	Late November	Royal Command Performance	Drury Lane Theatre or the London Palladium
	30 November or nearest Sunday	Thistle Service	St Giles's Cathedral, Edinburgh

REGULAR EVENTS

Daily	Changing of the Guard	Buckingham Palace, Whitehall, Horse Guards Parade, St James's Palace, Tower of London, Windsor
Nightly	Ceremony of the Keys	Tower of London

OCCASIONAL EVENTS

Every 4 years (next in 1986)	Bath Service	Westminster Abbey
Every 3 years (next in 1985)	Installation of new Governor of Edinburgh Castle	Edinburgh Castle Esplanade

Maps

On all the maps, place
names in bold are
mentioned in the text

Inverness

Crathie
Braemar **Balmoral** Aberdeen

Dundee
Perth

Glasgow
Edinburgh

Belfast

Newcastle
Durham

Dublin

Lancaster
Preston York
Bradford Leeds
Hull
Liverpool
Manchester
Caernarvon
Chester Sheffield

Lincoln
Nottingham

Aberystwyth
Birmingham Leicester **Sandringham**

Norwich
Worcester Stratford on Avon
Cambridge
Swansea Gloucester
Ipswich
Cardiff **Badminton**
Oxford **St Albans**
Bristol **Windsor**
Bath **Ascot**
Sandhurst **London**
Epsom
Winchester
Exeter Southampton Dover
Portsmouth **Hastings**
Plymouth
Brighton
Penzance

173

London

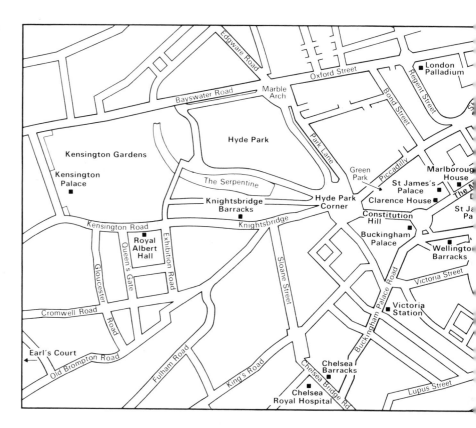

Edinburgh

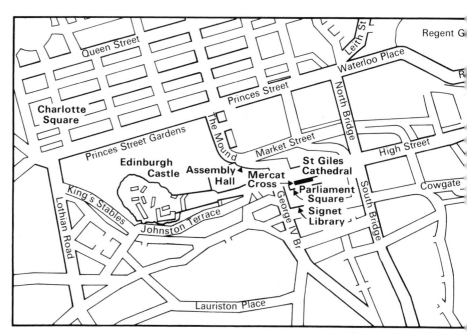

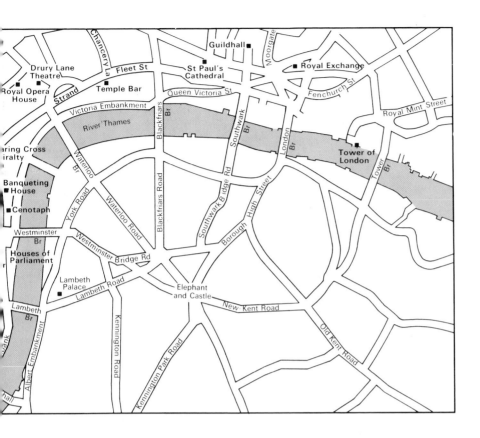

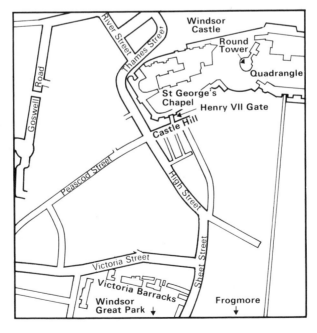

Windsor

Addresses

When applying in writing for tickets or information always send a stamped self-addressed envelope

British Tourist Authority
64 St James's Street, London SW1
Telephone 01-499 9325

Scottish Tourist Authority
23 Ravelstone Terrace, Edinburgh EH4 3EU
Telephone 031-332 2433

Welsh Tourist Authority
3 Castle Street, Cardiff CF1 2RE
Telephone 0222-27281

Windsor Tourist Authority
Central Station, Windsor. Berks
Telephone 07535-52010
(code from London is 95)

City of London Information Centre
St Paul's Churchyard, London EC4
Telephone 01-606 3030

London Tourist Board Information Centre
26 Grosvenor Gardens, London SW1
Telephone 01-730 0791

The Royal Tournament
For information regarding tickets
Telephone 01-371 8141

Edinburgh Military Tattoo
For tickets apply in writing from 1 January
and in person from first week in July, to
Tattoo Office, 1 Cockburn Street,
Edinburgh EH1 1QB
Telephone 031-225 1188

Ceremony of the Keys
For tickets apply in advance to
The Governor, The Tower of London,
Tower Hill, London EC3 4AB

Trooping the Colour
For tickets apply in writing for ballot
form 1 January-28 February to
The Brigade Major, Headquarters,
Household Division, Horse Guards,
Whitehall, London SW1A 2AX

Beating Retreat
For tickets apply to
The Ticket Centre, 1b Bridge Street,
Westminster, London SW1
Telephone 01-839 6815

Festival of Remembrance
For tickets for afternoon performance
apply to
Royal British Legion, 49 Pall Mall,
London SW1Y 5JY
Telephone 01-930 8131

Service of The Order of the Garter
For tickets apply in writing beginning of
January to
The Lord Chamberlain's Office,
St James's Palace, London SW1

Service of The Order of the Thistle
For tickets apply in writing to
The Dean of St Giles,
St Giles's Cathedral, Edinburgh

Royal Ascot
For tickets to the Royal Enclosure
apply in writing by end of April to
Her Majesty's Representative,
Ascot Office, St James's Palace,
London SW1
and for tickets for the Race Meeting
Telephone 0990-22211

Badminton Horse Trials
For details, including current ticket
prices, apply in writing to
Horse Trials Office, Badminton, Avon

Derby Day, Epsom
For details, including current ticket
prices, apply in writing to
United Race Courses,
Race Course Paddock, Epsom, Surrey

Braemar, the Royal Highland Gathering
For tickets apply early January
Telephone 03383-248

Occasional Events, State Visits
For dates and times see *The Times* 'Court
Circular' and 'Today's Events', and *Daily
Telegraph* 'Court and Social'

Whitaker's Almanack is an invaluable
annual source of dates, opening times and
addresses, as well as miscellaneous
information about the Royal Family

Index